EXAM QUESTION PRACTICE PACK

OCR GCSE (9–1)
COMPUTER SCIENCE

HODDER
EDUCATION
AN HACHETTE UK COMPANY

Hachette UK's policy is to use papers that are natural, renewable and recyclable products and made from wood grown in well-managed forests and other controlled sources. The logging and manufacturing processes are expected to conform to the environmental regulations of the country of origin.

Orders: please contact Hachette UK Distribution, Hely Hutchinson Centre, Milton Road, Didcot, Oxfordshire, OX11 7HH. Telephone: (44) 01235 827827. Email education@hachette.co.uk Lines are open from 9 a.m. to 5 p.m., Monday to Friday. You can also order through our website:

www.hoddereducation.co.uk

ISBN: 978 1 5104 3357 1

© Hodder & Stoughton 2018

First published in 2018 by
Hodder Education,
An Hachette UK Company
Carmelite House
50 Victoria Embankment
London EC4Y 0DZ

Impression number   10 9 8 7 6

Year   2023

Cover photo: Fotolia/Edelweiss

Typeset in India by Aptara Inc.

Printed in the UK

A catalogue record for this title is available from the British Library.

www.carbonbalancedprint.com
CBP2250

CONTENTS

Introduction

Exam questions

Component 1: Computer systems

Component 2: Computational thinking, algorithms and programming

Example responses and mark schemes

Component 1: Computer systems

Component 2: Computational thinking, algorithms and programming

INTRODUCTION

This pack of exam-style questions, example responses and mark schemes is specially curated for the OCR GCSE (9–1) Computer Science specification. The pack is divided into two sections:

➤ **Exam questions**. A bank of questions similar to those found in OCR GCSE (9–1) Computer Science papers. These are arranged in the order of topics in the specification. You may wish to photocopy all or part of them for use with your class.

➤ **Example responses and mark schemes**. For each question there are two student responses — a 'Student A' response typical of an answer receiving a high mark, and a 'Student B' response that would receive fewer marks. Each response includes examiner-style commentary which describes why it receives the marks it does. The mark scheme for each question indicates how these responses could be graded, and can be used alongside each type of student answer or just with the question.

The pack is designed to help you to:

➤ encourage students to reflect on their responses and ensure they know how to succeed

➤ cultivate students' key skills and knowledge by regular assessment throughout the course, or in the revision period before the exams

➤ incorporate question practice into your lesson plans in the final, vital stage of teaching a topic: putting theory into practice

➤ teach flexibly, choosing photocopiable pages as appropriate to share with students

➤ facilitate peer discussion of what is good or better about given answers, which allows greater insight into quality responses

➤ allow students to analyse responses without the bias that can come from looking at their own or their friends' work — and so get more from the task

EXAM QUESTIONS

Component 1 Computer systems

1.1 Systems architecture

1   The Central Processing Unit (CPU) may also be referred to as the processor or microprocessor.

(a) State three steps the CPU continuously carries out in a cycle when processing a program.

(3 marks)

....

....

....

(b) Describe an action the CPU might carry out during its execute phase.   **(2 marks)**

....

....

....

(c) The CPU uses the following to perform certain of its functions:
   ▷ address bus
   ▷ data bus
   ▷ control bus
   Give the function carried out by each.   **(6 marks)**

....

....

....

....

....

....

Total: 11 marks

(Example student responses and mark scheme on p. 68)

2   A Central Processing Unit (CPU) executes programs that are stored in memory.

  (a) Rebecca has bought a new computer which is capable of parallel processing. Describe how parallel processing works and how this will benefit Rebecca. **(3 marks)**

....

....

....

  (b) A CPU uses three steps in order to run a program: fetch, decode and execute. Complete the following table to explain what happens at each step. **(3 marks)**

Steps	Explanation
Fetch	
Decode	
Execute	

  (c) The clock speed of the CPU is measured in cycles per second. If one cycle per second is known as 1 hertz (1 Hz), state how many GHz a clock runs at if it runs at 4000 million cycles a second. **(1 mark)**

....

Total: 7 marks

(Example student responses and mark scheme on p. 70)

3   A register in a CPU is a place where a small amount of data can be held temporarily.

  (a) Describe what is held in the Memory Address Register (MAR). **(2 marks)**

....

....

  (b) Another register is the Memory Data Register (MDR). State the purpose of an MDR. **(2 marks)**

....

....

(c) Complete the following table to show whether the purpose is related to an MDR or an MAR. (4 marks)

Purpose	MDR or MAR?
CPU register where data to be transferred to or from memory are stored temporarily	
CPU register where the address of a memory location is kept so that data can be written to or read from it	
It is connected to the address bus	
It contains the data/instruction after a fetch from the computer storage	

Total: 8 marks

(Example student responses and mark scheme on p. 72)

4   A register in a CPU is a place where a small amount of data can be held temporarily. An example of a register is the MAR.

(a) Give the full name of the MAR. (1 mark)

....

(b) Give the purpose of the MAR. (3 marks)

....

....

....

Total: 4 marks

(Example student responses and mark scheme on p. 73)

5   In computing, small storage areas are built into the CPU to hold temporary data such as an address or an instruction.

(a) State what the Program Counter, Memory Address Register and Accumulator are all examples of. (1 mark)

....

(b) Explain the role of the Program Counter. (1 mark)

....

....

(c) Complete the following table with the name of the item that corresponds to each definition. **(4 marks)**

Name	Definition
	A set of instructions for a computer to perform
	An order/instruction within the program for the computer processor to carry out
	A specific location in memory or storage
	A small set of locations to hold data that the processor uses

Total: 6 marks

(Example student responses and mark scheme on p. 74)

6   The program counter is a register in the Central Processing Unit (CPU).
(a) Describe what is held in the program counter. **(1 mark)**

....

(b) The program counter holds the address of the current instruction. Explain what happens once that instruction has been fetched. **(4 marks)**

....

....

....

....

Total: 5 marks

(Example student responses and mark scheme on p. 75)

7   Without a register like an accumulator the result of each calculation would need to be sent to main memory. Describe how time is saved by using an accumulator rather than main memory to store intermediate arithmetic and logic results. **(6 marks)**

....

....

....

....

....

....

Total: 6 marks

(Example student responses and mark scheme on p. 76)

8   The mathematician John von Neumann conceived the computer architecture that bears his name in 1945. This architecture now forms the basis of nearly every computer system in use today, no matter what its size.

(a) State which three of the following are components of a Central Processing Unit (CPU). **(3 marks)**

> Registers
> Fetch
> Decode
> Control Unit
> Arithmetic Logic Unit
> Execute

....

....

....

(b) Mathematical and logical computations are carried out by the ALU. Give two examples. **(2 marks)**

....

....

(c) Look at Figure 1, which represents von Neumann architecture.

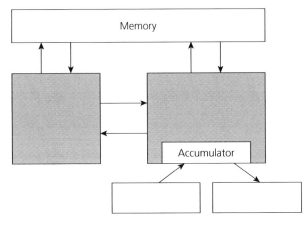

Figure 1

(i) Label the two shaded boxes in the centre of the diagram. **(2 marks)**

....

....

(ii) Label the two small boxes at the bottom of the diagram. (2 marks)

....

....

Total: 9 marks

(Example student responses and mark scheme on p. 77)

9   Von Neumann architecture is an example of a stored program architecture. Its essential features are:

➢ memory
➢ Control Unit
➢ Registers
➢ input and output
➢ Arithmetic Logic Unit (ALU)
➢ bus

Describe the essential features of von Neumann architecture, including their role and how information is passed between them. (10 marks)

....

....

....

....

....

....

....

....

....

Total: 10 marks

(Example student responses and mark scheme on p. 79)

10   The Central Processing Unit (CPU) is the control centre, or 'brain', of the computer. Three important components of the CPU are the Arithmetic Logic Unit (ALU), the Control Unit (CU) and registers. Describe the role of each of these components.   **(6 marks)**

....

....

....

....

....

....

....

Total: 6 marks

(Example student responses and mark scheme on p. 80)

11   The Arithmetic Logic Unit (ALU), Control Unit (CU), Memory Address Register (MAR) and Memory Data Register (MDR) are all components of the Central Processing Unit. Different tasks are listed in the table. Insert a tick (✔) to indicate which component carries out each task.   **(8 marks)**

	ALU	CU	MAR	MDR
It carries out arithmetic and logic comparison functions				
It makes decisions and sends the appropriate signal to other parts of the computer				
It provides a temporary memory storage location within the processor				
It carries out all the calculations and makes decisions on the data sent to the processor				
It controls the timing of operations in the computer and controls the instructions sent to the processor and the peripheral devices				
It manages all of the computer's resources				
It holds the address of the location to be fetched or stored				
It holds the data value being fetched or stored				

Total: 8 marks

(Example student responses and mark scheme on p. 81)

12 For a program to run, the Central Processing Unit (CPU) has to start by getting the first instruction in the program, i.e. begin the fetch, decode, execute cycle.

(a) The following list of tasks is not in sequence. Give the correct sequence by labelling the statements in the correct order that they are carried out, starting with A. The first one has been done for you.　　　　　　　　　　　　　　　　　　　　　　　**(6 marks)**

	The CPU sends a signal to all other hardware so the instruction is then executed
	The stored instruction is fetched from this address
A	The CPU has to get the first instruction in the program
	The instruction passes back to the CPU on the data bus
	The instruction is decoded by the CPU
	The instruction is fetched by putting it on the data bus
	The address of the instruction it wants to fetch is put on the address bus

(b) Complete the missing word in the following sentence:

A _____ is the term for the temporary memory in the processor where the ALU or the CU store and change the values needed to execute the instructions from the programs.　　　　　　　　　　　　　　　　　　　　　　　**(1 mark)**

Total: 7 marks

(Example student responses and mark scheme on p. 82)

13 The fetch-decode-execute cycle of a computer is repeated continuously by the Central Processing Unit (CPU); during this process many internal components are used. Some of the components used in the fetch-decode-execute cycle are listed below.

Write the correct component next to its definition in the table.　　　　　　**(4 marks)**

➢ Program counter
➢ Memory Address Register
➢ Control Unit
➢ Arithmetic Logic Unit

Component	Definition
	Carries out/performs mathematical operations and any logic comparisons
	The address in main memory currently being read or written
	It decodes the instruction given by the program
	This is incremental, meaning that it keeps track of memory addresses needed for the instruction to be executed next

Total: 4 marks

(Example student responses and mark scheme on p. 84)

14 Common characteristics of Central Processing Units (CPUs) can affect their performance.

(a) Imagine your work experience employer has asked you to advise on what affects the performance of the CPU. List the three common characteristics of CPUs that affect their performance. **(3 marks)**

....

....

....

(b) Explain why these three characteristics could affect the performance of a CPU. **(6 marks)**

....

....

....

....

....

....

Total: 9 marks

(Example student responses and mark scheme on p. 85)

15 Embedded systems perform predefined tasks within the device they control. There are examples of embedded systems in households, transport, industry, the military, consumer goods and many more.

(a) A personal computer is usually termed a general-purpose computer because it can perform many different types of task. An embedded computer carries out predefined tasks with specific requirements. Name two examples of an embedded system in telecommunications. **(2 marks)**

....

....

(b) Give the name for the type of program written for embedded systems. **(1 mark)**

....

(c) Many embedded systems must be safe and reliable. Give three examples, with reasons, of where it is absolutely necessary for them to be safe and reliable. **(6 marks)**

....

....

....

....

....

....

....

....

....

Total: 9 marks

(Example student responses and mark scheme on p. 86)

16　Embedded systems appear in many aspects of everyday life where they are located within the system that they control.

(a) Name three types of appliance in the home that are controlled by embedded systems.

(3 marks)

....

....

....

(b) Discuss the advantages and disadvantages of an embedded system. (10 marks)

....

....

....

....

....

....

....

....

Total: 13 marks

(Example student responses and mark scheme on p. 87)

1.2 Memory

1   Although there are a lot of differences between RAM and ROM, both RAM and ROM are types of memory used by a computer and they are both needed for your computer to operate properly and efficiently.

(a) State the full names of RAM and ROM.   (2 marks)

....

....

(b) Insert a tick (✓) to indicate whether each of the statements in the following table refers to RAM or ROM.   (8 marks)

	RAM	ROM
Memory available for the operating system and programs to use when the computer is running		
Memory that holds instructions for booting-up the computer		
Memory that requires the computer to be on in order to retain data		
Data are not permanently written to this type of memory		
It is a type of volatile memory		
Data in this type of memory are permanently written		
Data in this type of memory are not lost when the computer is switched off		
Data in this type of memory are pre-written and come with a computer		

(c) State where a ROM chip is likely to be located in a personal computer.   (1 mark)

....

Total: 11 marks

(Example student responses and mark scheme on p. 88)

2   ROM stores the instructions which the computer uses when it boots up.

(a) When the computer is switched on, or booted up, the BIOS carries out various checks. Give the full name of the BIOS.   (1 mark)

....

(b) State three checks that the BIOS carries out at start-up.   (3 marks)

....

....

....

Total: 4 marks

(Example student responses and mark scheme on p. 90)

3   The set of instructions on the Read-Only Memory (ROM) interact directly with various hardware components. Discuss the role of ROM in a computer system.   **(8 marks)**

....

....

....

....

....

....

....

Total: 8 marks

(Example student responses and mark scheme on p. 91)

4   Without memory, a computer would not be of much use.
    (a) State what is stored in memory.   **(1 mark)**

....

    (b) Random Access Memory (RAM) is a component in a computer that allows the system to perform frequent tasks such as loading applications, browsing, editing a spreadsheet, playing a game etc. Describe what happens inside RAM when you want to open a spreadsheet program, use a spreadsheet file to carry out some edits before saving and closing the file.   **(4 marks)**

....

....

....

....

Total: 5 marks

(Example student responses and mark scheme on p. 93)

5   RAM holds information that is essential for whatever is being done on the computer now. Insert a tick (✔) in the right-hand column in the following table to indicate which statements are correct.   **(4 marks)**

Statement	Correct?
RAM provides a workspace to store information that the processor is using	
Sometimes a portion of the hard drive is used as extra RAM space	
Hard drives are slower than RAM at transferring data	
RAM stands for Rapid Access Memory	
DRAM is the most common form of RAM	

Total 4 marks

(Example student responses and mark scheme on p. 94)

6   Virtual memory is a technique that uses hardware and software when the operating system controls the assignment of real memory to virtual memory.

(a) Which of the following types of memory may be used when a computer is swapping data in and out of virtual memory?   **(1 mark)**
   ▷ RAM and a hard disk drive
   ▷ RAM and cache memory
   ▷ A hard disk drive and cache memory

....

(b) Explain the process of swapping (sometimes called paging).   **(6 marks)**

....

....

....

....

....

(c) When swapping data in and out of virtual memory, data from RAM is transferred to and from a temporary file on a hard disk. Describe why this might be necessary.   **(6 marks)**

....

....

....

....

....

Total: 13 marks

(Example student responses and mark scheme on p. 95)

7   One of the components of an operating system is virtual memory. It allows more applications to run even if there is not enough physical memory to support them. Insert a tick (✓) in the following table to show if each statement is correct or incorrect.   **(4 marks)**

	Correct	Incorrect
Using virtual memory makes the computer run more quickly		
Virtual memory is a technique that only uses hardware		
Virtual memory is a technique that uses both hardware and software		
Copying to a hard disk takes longer than reading and writing to and from RAM		

Total: 4 marks

(Example student responses and mark scheme on p. 96)

8   Flash memory is a type of storage. It is often used in USB sticks for transferring data between computers.
   (a) From the following list, choose all the items that apply to flash memory.   **(4 marks)**
      ▷ Non-volatile   ▷ Storage medium
      ▷ Solid-state   ▷ Rewritable
      ▷ Volatile   ▷ Optical storage

   ....

   ....

   ....

   ....

   (b) Give four examples of where flash memory is used.   **(4 marks)**

   ....

   ....

   ....

   ....

Total: 8 marks

(Example student responses and mark scheme on p. 97)

1.3 Storage

1   Secondary storage allows data and programs to be stored even when a computer is turned off.

(a) Give two reasons, with appropriate examples, of why secondary storage is needed.   (4 marks)

....

....

....

....

(b) Give three common types of secondary storage.   (3 marks)

....

....

....

(c) Insert a tick (✔) in the appropriate cell in the following table to indicate which type of storage applies in each case.   (8 marks)

	Optical	Solid state	Magnetic
Blu-ray disk			
Hard disk			
CD			
Tablet PC			
Mobile phone			
DVD			
Camera memory card			
Tablet			

Total: 15 marks

(Example student responses and mark scheme on p. 98)

2   Storage and memory on a computer are measured in megabytes (MB) and gigabytes (GB). Complete the blank cells in the following table.

(6 marks)

Size	Binary power	Equal to	Common abbreviation
8 bits		1 byte	B
1024 bytes	2^{10}	1 kilobyte	kB
1024 kilobytes		1 megabyte	
1024 megabytes	2^{30}	1 gigabyte	GB
1024 gigabytes	2^{40}	1 terabyte	TB
1024 terabytes		1 petabyte	
1024 petabytes	2^{60}		EB
	2^{70}	1 zettabyte	ZB
1024 zettabytes	2^{80}	1 yottabyte	YB

Total 6 marks

(Example student responses and mark scheme on p. 100)

3   There are three main types of secondary storage: solid-state, magnetic and optical. They are all capable of long-term storage. Give two advantages and two disadvantages of solid-state, magnetic and optical storage.

(12 marks)

....

....

....

....

....

....

....

....

....

....

....

Total: 12 marks

(Example student responses and mark scheme on p. 102)

4   Storage devices are peripheral devices to a main computer system. The storage medium holds the data and the storage device allows data to be stored on the medium.

(a) List six considerations that you need establish before deciding on a suitable storage device. **(6 marks)**

....

....

....

....

....

....

(b) You want to be able to carry your data around with you between school or college and home. You have not decided yet whether to use a memory stick or a portable hard drive. Compare the advantages and disadvantages of using a memory stick/pen drive and a portable hard drive, then state which one is best for you. **(10 marks)**

....

....

....

....

....

....

....

....

....

....

....

Total: 16 marks

(Example student responses and mark scheme on p. 103)

5   Storage devices are peripheral devices to a main computer system. There are many different types and it is important to choose the best one for any particular situation.

(a) Explain the difference between a storage device and a storage medium. **(2 marks)**

....

....

(b) Complete the following table to explain what each term means in relation to storage devices in general. **(6 marks)**

Capacity	
Speed	
Durability	
Reliability	
Cost	
Portability	

(c) (i) Give the type of storage device that would be used by an organisation with a large volume of data. Speed of access is not important to them. **(1 mark)**

....

(ii) State the kind of data access that will be used by this device. **(1 mark)**

....

Total: 10 marks

(Example student responses and mark scheme on p. 104)

1.4 Wired and wireless networks

1   The types of network that you may have come across are referred to as a LAN, a WAN or a WLAN.

(a) Give the full names for each of the following:

(i) LAN **(1 mark)**

....

(ii) WAN **(1 mark)**

....

(iii) WLAN **(1 mark)**

....

(b) Describe how a WAN, a LAN and a WLAN differ from each other. **(6 marks)**

....

....

....

....

....

....

Total: 9 marks

(Example student responses and mark scheme on p. 106)

2   Networks are usually described as types of area networks which are a Local Area Network
     (LAN), a Wide Area Network (WAN) or a Wireless Local Area Network (WLAN).

     A shop selling musical instruments has several computers already and is thinking of joining
     the computers together into a network. The business may need to expand by opening
     other music shops in the future. It needs to decide which type of network is best in the
     circumstances: a LAN, a WAN or a WLAN.

     Describe the differences between the three network types and then state which would be
     most suitable.   **(5 marks)**

....

....

....

....

....

Total: 5 marks

(Example student responses and mark scheme on p. 107)

3   The performance of a computer network can be affected by a range of different factors that
     sometimes cause it to be slow.
     (a) State what determines the overall maximum possible speed of a network.   **(1 mark)**

....

     (b) For a broadband connection, state which has more bandwidth assigned to it:
         downloading or uploading. Give a reason for your response.   **(2 marks)**

....

....

     (c) Asymmetric digital subscriber line (ADSL) uses telephone lines to transmit and receive data.
         List two factors of ADSL that may affect the speed at which data can be transferred.   **(2 marks)**

....

....

Total: 5 marks

(Example student responses and mark scheme on p. 108)

4   There are different types of network and performance and their performance can vary widely.

   (a) Insert a tick (✓) in the following table to indicate whether each statement is true or false.

                                                                                           (6 marks)

CABLE broadband internet access	True	False
They do not use traditional telephone lines to provide broadband internet access		
Cable companies provide considerably more Mbps than are available with ADSL		
A cable modem or router is not necessary for broadband internet access over cable		
Cable networks are a combination of coaxial copper cable and fibre optic cable		
Making and receiving telephone calls will be affected by having cable broadband internet access		
Copper wires connect a house to the nearest connection point		

   (b) Explain the term 'bottleneck' in relation to speed of data transfer across an ADSL connection.

                                                                                           (3 marks)

....

....

....

Total: 9 marks

(Example student responses and mark scheme on p. 109)

5   There are many differences between client–server and peer-to-peer networks.

   (a) Insert a tick (✓) in the following table to indicate whether each statement relates to a peer-to-peer or a client–server network.

                                                                                        (8 marks)

	Peer-to-peer network	Client–server network
They have no central server		
Centralised security controls access to shared resources on servers		
Shared resources are kept on the server		
Each workstation on the network shares its files equally with the other workstations		
Access to shared resources on the server is controlled		
There is no authentication of users		
The server contains a list of usernames and passwords		
They offer better security		

(b) Describe the difference between the security on a client–server network and on a peer-to-peer network. **(2 marks)**

....

....

Total: 10 marks

(Example student responses and mark scheme on p. 111)

6   In a peer-to-peer network, each client can download and share files with other users. In a client–server network, a client depends on the server to manage the information.

(a) Draw a diagram of a peer-to-peer network. Show at least three peers and use arrows to indicate information flows. **(3 marks)**

(b) Draw a diagram of a client–server network. Show one client and one server, using arrows to indicate information flows. **(4 marks)**

Total: 7 marks

(Example student responses and mark scheme on p. 112)

7   Network devices are hardware components used to connect computers and other devices or peripherals together in a network. When they are connected, they are able to share files and resources within the network.

(a) In a network, one computer acts as the server and the other computers are called clients. State what item of hardware the server connects to that the client computers are also connected to. **(1 mark)**

....

(b) Name three other common devices used to set up a LAN. **(3 marks)**

....

....

....

(c) A modem is used to connect a computer to send and receive signals over a telephone line. Explain how a modem enables a signal from a computer to travel down a telephone line and back. (4 marks)

....

....

....

....

....

Total: 8 marks

(Example student responses and mark scheme on p. 114)

8 (a) Insert a tick (✔) in the following table to indicate whether the statement applies to switches or to routers. (5 marks)

	Switches	Routers
They can send and receive data at the same time		
They can pass data between two networks		
They send data only to the computer for which they are intended		
They provide built-in security such as a firewall		
They can be wireless		

(b) (i) Define WAP. (1 mark)

....

(ii) State what it provides. (1 mark)

....

Total: 7 marks

(Example student responses and mark scheme on p. 116)

9 There are many different items of hardware that may be needed to connect computers into a LAN. As well as hardware components, there are various transmission media to be considered.
(a) Give the full name of an NIC. (1 mark)

....

(b) Describe the purpose of an NIC. (2 marks)

....

....

(c) Name three examples of transmission media. (3 marks)

....

....

Total: 6 marks

(Example student responses and mark scheme on p. 117)

10 There are many different items of hardware that can be needed to connect computers into a LAN. As well as hardware components, there are various transmission media to be considered.
   (a) Name two items that you would need to allow your computer to connect to the internet wirelessly. (2 marks)

....

....

   (b) Discuss the advantages and disadvantages of wireless networks. (8 marks)

....

....

....

....

....

....

Total: 10 marks

(Example student responses and mark scheme on p. 118)

11 A DNS server plays a key role in routing you to the URL you require when browsing the internet.
   (a) Give the full name of DNS. (1 mark)

....

   (b) Explain the role of a DNS server. (4 marks)

....

....

....

Total: 5 marks

(Example student responses and mark scheme on p. 119)

12 Describe what an Internet Protocol (IP) address is and what it is used for. **(2 marks)**

....

....

Total: 2 marks

(Example student responses and mark scheme on p. 120)

13 The World Wide Web is a collection of online content accessible via the internet.
   (a) Explain why you might need a web hosting service. **(1 mark)**

....

   (b) Describe four factors that would help you to decide which hosting company to use for your website. **(8 marks)**

....

....

....

....

....

....

....

Total: 9 marks

(Example student responses and mark scheme on p. 120)

14 One of the provisions of cloud computing is that you are able to access and use applications that are stored on remote servers, rather than on your own computer.
   (a) Cloud computing is used to access and use applications such as word processors, databases and spreadsheets. Give two other ways in which you could use cloud computing. **(2 marks)**

....

....

   (b) Describe the advantages to businesses and individuals of using cloud computing. **(4 marks)**

....

....

....

....

Total: 6 marks

(Example student responses and mark scheme on p. 121)

15 Cloud computing has become ever more popular and brings with it its own advantages and disadvantages to the user.

    (a) Some government departments, banks or financial institutions, among others, may wish to create their own cloud servers rather than publically available ones. Give two reasons why an organisation may choose to store data on a privately owned cloud server.   **(2 marks)**

....

....

    (b) Discuss the advantages and disadvantages of cloud computing.   **(10 marks)**

....

....

....

....

....

....

....

....

....

....

Total: 12 marks

(Example student responses and mark scheme on p. 122)

16 A virtual network makes it possible to interact with a computer from a mobile device or a computer that is on the internet.

    (a) State what is meant by virtual networking.   **(3 marks)**

....

....

....

(b) Insert a tick (✓) in the following table to show whether each statement is true or false. **(4 marks)**

	True	False
A VLAN is configured through software		
A virtual network link is neither a wired nor a wireless connection		
You cannot store or retrieve data over a virtual network		
Virtual networking is a standard feature of some versions of MS Windows		

Total: 7 marks

(Example student responses and mark scheme on p. 124)

17 A virtual network allows interaction with computers and devices from a mobile device or a computer that is on the internet, giving the appearance that all of the computers and devices are on the same site. Give two advantages of virtual networking. **(2 marks)**

....

....

Total: 2 marks

(Example student responses and mark scheme on p. 125)

1.5 Network topologies, protocols and layers

1 Network topology is the arrangement of the elements that make up a computer network.
 (a) Name the two different network topologies shown in Figure 2. **(2 marks)**

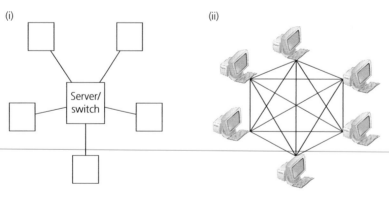

Figure 2

....

....

 (b) Using Figure 2, list two advantages and two disadvantages of each type of topology. **(8 marks)**

....

....

....

....

....

....

....

Total: 10 marks

(Example student responses and mark scheme on p. 126)

2   Network topology is a description of connections between the components of a network

    (a) Draw and describe a star topology.   **(5 marks)**

....

....

    (b) Draw and describe a mesh topology.   **(5 marks)**

....

....

Total: 10 marks

(Example student responses and mark scheme on p. 127)

3   WiFi stands for 'wireless fidelity'. WiFi allows computers, smartphones and other wireless devices to connect to the internet and to communicate with one another wirelessly within a particular area.

(a) Fill in the blank spaces in the following sentences using the following terms:

radio   router   wireless   Wireless Network Interface Card

Wireless networks use _____ waves.

In a WiFi network, the device that sends and receives radio signals is the

_____

A _____ router should be centrally placed in your home for the best possible range.

Most laptops have a _____ built in.   (4 marks)

(b) Insert a tick (✓) in the following table to indicate whether each statement is true or false.   (7 marks)

Statements	True	False
A WiFi network is faster than a cabled network		
The speed of a WiFi network is influenced by the strength of the radio signal		
A wireless router cannot make a connection with a physical network		
A WiFi connection is more stable than a wired network		
A wireless adaptor converts data into a radio signal		
A wireless receiver also converts data into a radio signal		
It costs a lot less to add extra hardware to a WiFi network		

(c) Compare the advantages and disadvantages of a wireless network.   (8 marks)

....

....

....

....

....

....

....

....

Total: 19 marks

(Example student responses and mark scheme on p. 130)

4   Ethernet is the most popular physical layer for LAN technology.

(a) Define the term 'ethernet'.   (2 marks)

....

....

(b) Ethernet provides a framework for data transmission. State two standards that it defines.
                                                                                                   (2 marks)

....

....

(c) Make a list of what makes ethernet a popular networking technology for most
computer users.   (8 marks)

....

....

....

....

....

....

....

....

Total: 12 marks

(Example student responses and mark scheme on p. 132)

5   A protocol is the set of rules for a telecommunications connection.

(a) In the following table, write a definition and a description for each acronym.   (10 marks)

Acronym	Definition	Description
TCP/IP		
FTP		
POP		
IMAP		
SMTP		

(b) TCP/IP networks use both MAC addresses and IP addresses for different purposes. Give the main difference between a MAC address and an IP address. **(2 marks)**

....

....

(c) Describe the main differences between http:// and https://. **(4 marks)**

....

....

....

....

Total: 16 marks

(Example student responses and mark scheme on p. 133)

6   Networked computers must have a method of being able to communicate with each other. They do this by following the same protocol.

   (a) List a typical set of rules that are defined by a protocol. **(6 marks)**

....

....

....

....

....

....

   (b) TCP/IP is the protocol in use on most LANs and the internet. Describe the function of TCP and IP. **(2 marks)**

....

....

   (c) Explain how data packets travel and why they have to be put into the right order once they arrive at their destination. **(6 marks)**

....

....

....

....

....

....

Total: 14 marks

(Example student responses and mark scheme on p. 135)

7   In the TCP/IP protocol suite there are four layers. Each layer has a set of data that it generates.

    (a) Name the four layers in the TCP/IP protocol.   **(4 marks)**

....

....

....

....

    (b) In the following table, give the correct layer name for each description.   **(4 marks)**

Description	Layer name
The MAC address information to specify sending and receiving hardware devices	
It encodes the data being transmitted	
Adds the IP addresses of the sender and recipient	
The data is divided into manageable chunks	

    (c) Describe the benefits of using networking layers.   **(5 marks)**

....

....

....

....

Total: 13 marks

(Example student responses and mark scheme on p. 136)

8   Data packets travel from their source to their destination by being passed on from one router to the next. This process for exchanging data packets is called packet switching.

    (a) Each data packet contains standard fields. Apart from the data, name five of the standard fields contained in a data packet.   **(5 marks)**

....

....

....

(b) Explain how data packets travel through the network. (8 marks)

(c) Give three advantages of packet switching. (3 marks)

Total: 16 marks

(Example student responses and mark scheme on p. 138)

1.6 System security

1   Penetration testing, or pen testing, will help to reveal problems that were previously unknown. Describe the main reasons for performing penetration testing. (7 marks)

Total: 7 marks

(Example student responses and mark scheme on p. 139)

2   Network policies are a set of rules (constraints) that authorised users must comply with to be allowed to connect to a network. Some organisations also employ network forensics to help to keep their IT infrastructure secure.

(a) Define 'network forensics'. (2 marks)

....

....

(b) Describe four ways in which an organisation could use network forensics. (4 marks)

....

....

....

....

(c) Add words to the blank boxes in Figure 3 to state the main issues that would be covered in a typical network policy. (5 marks)

Figure 3

Total: 11 marks

(Example student responses and mark scheme on p. 140)

3   Malware is code created to do something malicious to your computer. Usually, it infiltrates a person's computer system without their knowledge.

(a) Anti-malware software is software that you can install on a computer to protect your system from malware infiltration and infection. Describe what anti-malware software does. (3 marks)

....

....

....

(b) Explain what a firewall is. (7 marks)

....

....

....

....

....

....

(c) Compare the main features of anti-malware software and a firewall. (10 marks)

....

....

....

....

....

....

....

....

....

....

Total: 20 marks

(Example student responses and mark scheme on p. 142)

4 Network managers are always looking for ways to keep the network secure and employing user access levels is one of the ways that helps.

(a) State what is meant by levels of access. (2 marks)

....

....

(b) Insert a tick (✓) in the following table to indicate whether each permission is applicable to a network manager or to a user. **(6 marks)**

Type of permission	Network manager	User
Install software		
Remove software		
Can only access particular software stored in work area		
Access all user area		
Change permissions		
Can manage account users		

(c) Michael is a network manager. He has to decide on access levels for users. List some of the items that he will have to decide upon. **(4 marks)**

....

....

....

....

Total: 12 marks

(Example student responses and mark scheme on p. 144)

5 Passwords are one way of keeping a network secure. Michelle is the marketing manager for a company selling sportswear. State the reasons she needs to enter a username and password to access the company's network. **(5 marks)**

....

....

....

....

....

Total: 5 marks

(Example student responses and mark scheme on p. 146)

6 Online security is a major concern, especially when you're using the internet to send sensitive information between parties. Encryption in various forms has been used for thousands of years and nowadays it is used when sending digital data over the internet.

(a) Explain what is meant by data encryption. **(2 marks)**

....

....

(b) Explain what is meant by data decryption. **(1 mark)**

....

....

(c) Explain how public-key encryption, also known as asymmetric encryption, works. **(10 marks)**

....

....

....

....

....

....

....

....

....

....

....

Total: 13 marks

(Example student responses and mark scheme on p. 146)

7   Giving away secure information can cause loss of data, lack of privacy and the loss of personal information.

(a) Study Figure 4. Write the labels for the four empty shapes in the diagram with the names of different types of malware. **(4 marks)**

Figure 4

(b) Explain what is meant by phishing. **(3 marks)**

....

....

....

(c) Social engineering is another form of attack. Describe how it attempts to gain information from a person using an otherwise secure system. **(4 marks)**

....

....

....

....

Total: 11 marks

(Example student responses and mark scheme on p. 148)

8 Brute-force attacks can be used against any type of encryption, but success is sometimes limited

(a) Explain how a brute-force attack attempts to break into a computer system. **(2 marks)**

....

....

(b) Describe the different methods that attempt to prevent brute-force attacks. **(3 marks)**

....

....

....

(c) State the different events that might make you suspicious that a brute-force attack had been attempted. **(5 marks)**

....

....

....

....

....

Total: 10 marks

(Example student responses and mark scheme on p. 149)

9 When you type a URL for a particular site into your browser, you are actually sending a request to that site's server to view the page on your computer, but sometimes it cannot process your request.

(a) Name the kind of attack that could be taking place when this happens. **(1 mark)**

....

(b) Describe the features of this attack. (7 marks)

....

....

....

....

....

....

(c) State two methods of reducing the risk of this type of attack. (2 marks)

....

....

Total: 10 marks

(Example student responses and mark scheme on p. 150)

10 There are several types of security problem that may be encountered on a network.
   (a) Software can intercept and log data passing through a network. State what this software is
   commonly known as. (1 mark)

....

   (b) (i) Give the full name of SQL. (1 mark)

....

   (ii) Explain how an SQL injection can destroy a database. (5 marks)

....

....

....

....

....

Total: 7 marks

(Example student responses and mark scheme on p. 152)

11 A network security policy is a company's document outlining its strategy for maintaining
   confidentiality, integrity and availability of network assets.
   (a) Write a sentence to best describe each of the following three security objectives:
   (i) confidentiality (1 mark)

....

(ii) integrity (1 mark)

....

(iii) availability (1 mark)

....

(b) A poor network policy could result in threats posed to the network. Figure 5 gives a list of various possible threats to a network. Write a description of each one in the empty boxes. (9 marks)

PHISHING	
SNIFFER ATTACK	
PASSWORD-BASED ATTACK	
DENIAL OF SERVICE ATTACK	
FORMS OF ATTACK ON NETWORKS → BRUTE-FORCE ATTACK	
SQL INJECTION	
POOR NETWORK POLICY	
MALWARE	
PEOPLE AS THE WEAK POINT IN A SECURE SYSTEM	

Figure 5

Total: 12 marks

(Example student responses and mark scheme on p. 153)

12 Penetration testing, or pen testing, is attempting to evaluate the security of a computer system by looking for, and trying to exploit, any areas where it is vulnerable.

(a) State the main difference between a penetration tester and a hacker. (1 mark)

....

(b) Name the four stages in the procedure for pen testing. **(4 marks)**

....

....

....

....

Total: 5 marks

(Example student responses and mark scheme on p. 155)

1.7 Systems software

1   An operating system is an essential piece of software on modern computer systems.

(a) Describe the following ways of interacting with your operating system:
  ➢ graphical user interface (GUI)
  ➢ command line interface (CLI) **(4 marks)**

....

....

....

....

(b) Using the following table, compare the differences between using a CLI and using a GUI.

(10 marks)

Comparisons	CLI	GUI
User-friendliness		
Diversity		
Multi-tasking		
Speed of operating		
System resources		

Total: 14 marks

(Example student responses and mark scheme on p. 156)

2   The operating system creates an interface between you and the hardware but it also has many other features.

(a) List six features that an operating system includes.   (6 marks)

....

....

....

....

....

....

(b) Define the terms in the following table.   (6 marks)

Term	Definition
Command line interface	
Device driver	
Utilities	
Linker	
Graphical user interface	
Compiler	

Total: 12 marks

(Example student responses and mark scheme on p. 159)

3   An operating system allocates space for files in secondary storage. However, there is no guarantee that a file can be stored contiguously on a physical disk drive.

(a) The following sentences give some of the actions of the operating system. Fill in the blank spaces in the sentences using the terms below.   (8 marks)

backing store   interface   peripherals   memory
processing time   programs   errors   security

Controls _____ such as scanners and printers.

Responsible for the transfer of programs in and out of _____.

Organises the use of memory between _____.

Organises _____ _____ between programs and users.

Maintains _____ and users' access rights.

Deals with _____ and user instructions.

Allows the user to save files to a _____ _____.

Provides an _____ between the user and the computer.

(b) Study Figure 6. When a file is updated it may become larger and require more unallocated space in memory than there is available in one place. Explain how the file manager would allocate space to that file now that it is larger. Refer to Figure 6 if you wish. **(4 marks)**

Allocated memory

Unallocated memory

Figure 6

....

....

....

....

Total: 12 marks

(Example student responses and mark scheme on p. 160)

4   A multi-tasking operating system allows multiple processes to take place at the same time.

(a) Operating systems can allow multi-tasking. Explain what is meant by multi-tasking and how the operating system works to achieve this. **(8 marks)**

....

....

....

....

....

....

....

(b) Describe how an operating system manages memory. **(4 marks)**

....

....

....

....

Total: 12 marks

(Example student responses and mark scheme on p. 162)

5   File management includes methods of reorganising files.

   (a) List five tasks that can be carried out to organise files.   **(5 marks)**

....

....

....

....

....

   (b) State what happens when files are transferred from one folder to another on the same disk.   **(1 mark)**

....

Total: 6 marks

(Example student responses and mark scheme on p. 163)

6   There are several utilities to let users manage files. Usually, the files are organised into a hierarchical system of folders or directories. There is usually a main folder which contains files or more folders. These folders can also contain other files and folders.

   (a) Insert a tick (✔) in the following table to indicate which two of the actions are carried out when you transfer a file from one folder to another on the same disk.   **(2 marks)**

	FAT is updated
	User moves or copies and pastes the file to new folder
	File is physically moved

   (b) List five areas that a multi-user operating system has to manage for those users.   **(5 marks)**

....

....

....

....

....

Total: 7 marks

(Example student responses and mark scheme on p. 164)

7 Utility software has programs that help to make your computer work more efficiently or add functionality.

(a) Insert a tick (✓) in the following table to indicate those that are utility software. **(5 marks)**

	Utility software?
Anti-virus software	
Applications software such as spreadsheets	
Bootloader	
Security programs	
Network programs	
Disk repair	
BIOS	
Backup facilities	

(b) Using the following list of utilities, fill in the table by inserting each utility next to its description. **(6 marks)**

Backup utility   **File viewer**   **Compression**   **Screen saver**
Diagnostic utility   **Disk defragmenter**

Utility	Description
	To display the contents of a file
	Reorganises files and unused space on a disk
	To shrink the size of a file
	Copies files or an entire disk onto another disk or tape
	Compiles technical information about a computer and reports on any identified problems
	Shows a moving image on screen when no keyboard activity has occurred for a specific time

Total: 11 marks

(Example student responses and mark scheme on p. 165)

8 Using encryption is a good way to protect your data. Explain what is meant by encryption.
(4 marks)

....

....

....

....

Total: 4 marks

(Example student responses and mark scheme on p. 167)

9   Utility software can carry out a lot of common tasks and is often built into the operating system.

(a) State what defragmentation means.   (2 marks)

....

....

(b) State why it is better to have the data on a storage device held contiguously rather than discontiguously.   (2 marks)

....

....

Total: 4 marks

(Example student responses and mark scheme on p. 168)

10 When you want to achieve faster transmission times for electronic files, you can compress them. This will result in the data using a lower number of bytes to store and then transmit (and download) the file.

(a) State which types of compression are shown in Figures 7 and 8.   **(1 mark)**

File before compression   Compressed   Restored file

Figure 7

File before compression   Compressed   Restored file

Figure 8

....

....

(b) Explain the difference between lossy and lossless compression.   **(4 marks)**

....

....

....

....

Total: 5 marks

(Example student responses and mark scheme on p. 169)

11   The role of backup is an important one and it should be carried out regularly.
      (a) Name the two main types of backup.   (2 marks)

....

....

      (b) Name four possible types of backup media.   (4 marks)

....

....

....

....

Total: 6 marks

(Example student responses and mark scheme on p. 170)

12   Computer data must be backed up and there are different methods that can be used when
      backing up. Describe the differences between the two main types of backup.
      (a) Incremental backup   (2 marks)

....

....

      (b) Full backup   (2 marks)

....

....

Total: 4 marks

(Example student responses and mark scheme on p. 171)

1.8 Ethical, legal, cultural and environmental concerns

1   Computer systems, and the use of them, can raise ethical issues that are not covered by the law. Ethics are about the standards that govern conduct in relationships with others. Computer ethics relate to the conduct of an individual in relation to computer systems as a whole.

(a) Denise is writing a textbook for computer science that will be sold worldwide. Describe the types of ethical issues that she will have to think about to ensure she is considerate to others when writing.   (8 marks)

....

....

....

....

....

....

....

(b) Discuss the term 'hacking' and how it may be used for negative as well as for positive purposes.   (8 marks)

....

....

....

....

....

....

....

....

(c) Insert a tick (✔) in the following table if the statement is an ethical issue. **(3 marks)**

	✓ if an ethical issue
Your boss can read your work-related and your private emails sent during work time	
You have written a new app and given a copy to your friend who is using it without paying for it	
A teacher of a new subject has a responsibility to make sure they can do the job by getting trained in that subject	
A car crashes because of a problem with an embedded computer in a production run	

Total: 19 marks

(Example student responses and mark scheme on p. 172)

2 Ethical considerations affect many areas of computing including privacy, sharing, hacking and the environment.

(a) Technology can impact on the environment to its advantage and to its disadvantage. Describe three benefits and three drawbacks that new technology has on the environment. **(6 marks)**

....

....

....

....

....

....

(b) As the use of computers for social networking has increased, so have the opportunities to misuse them.

(i) Define cyberbullying. **(2 marks)**

....

....

(ii) Define trolling. **(2 marks)**

....

....

Total: 10 marks

(Example student responses and mark scheme on p. 174)

3   Two types of software available are: proprietary and open source.

(a) Define open source software.   (1 mark)

....

....

(b) (i) List the advantages and disadvantages of open source software.   (6 marks)

Advantages	Disadvantages

(ii) List the advantages and disadvantages of proprietary software.   (6 marks)

Advantages	Disadvantages

(c) Insert a tick (✓) in the following table to indicate whether each item of software is proprietary or open source.   (6 marks)

	Proprietary	Open source
Mozilla Firefox		
Linux		
MS Office		
Adobe Photoshop		
Apache		
WordPress		

Total: 19 marks

(Example student responses and mark scheme on p. 176)

4   As technology and the internet rapidly evolve, new ethical and legal dilemmas emerge and
    there are laws in place to govern the use of computers as well as the internet.

    (a) The Computer Misuse Act is one of the laws that helps to govern legal issues. State what
        the Computer Misuse Act makes illegal.   (3 marks)

    ....

    ....

    ....

    (b) Complete the following table by inserting the name of the law to which each
        statement applies.   (5 marks)

	Organisations that store personal data on a computer system must have processes and security mechanisms
	Employers are responsible for appropriate working conditions of staff
	If you store personal details about others, they must be kept secure
	It is illegal to use software unless you buy the appropriate licence
	It is illegal to alter data without permission

    (c) The Data Protection Act controls how personal information may be used and everyone
        responsible for using data must follow very strict rules called the data protection principles.
        List as many of the eight data protection principles as you can.   (8 marks)

    ....

    ....

    ....

    ....

    ....

    ....

    ....

    ....

    Total: 16 marks

    (Example student responses and mark scheme on p. 178)

5   Creative Commons (CC) gives creators a way of sharing their work without having to give up copyright, and without having to individually license their work. CC licences have provided the public with a way to use works under set circumstances.

    (a) Define a CC licence.   (1 mark)

....

....

    (b) Name four key issues of CC licences.   (4 marks)

....

....

....

....

Total: 5 marks

(Example student responses and mark scheme on p. 180)

6   The Freedom of Information Act gives the public the right of access to information held by public authorities.

    (a) Name four public bodies that may have to give greater openness and accountability under this Act.   (4 marks)

....

....

....

....

    (b) Does the Freedom of Information Act apply to information held before the Act came into being?   (1 mark)

....

    (c) Name three types of recorded information included under the Act.   (3 marks)

....

....

....

Total: 8 marks

(Example student responses and mark scheme on p. 181)

Component 2: Computational thinking, algorithms and programming

2.1 Algorithms

1   (a) A single dimensional array contains ten names (defined as array names [10]). Using a flowchart, design an algorithm to:
   ▷ input a target name
   ▷ perform a linear search of the array name, checking to see if target name is in the array
   ▷ return true if target name is found else return false   **(6 marks)**

   (b) Explain how the following list of numbers is sorted using a merge sort:
   54, 26, 93, 17   **(5 marks)**

   (c) George was asked to design an algorithm for a bubble sort that sorts an array of names into alphabetical order. He started to write the algorithm using pseudocode, but has now left the company. Finish the algorithm.   **(5 marks)**

```
procedure bubblesort (listOfNames, numberOfElements)
   i = 0
   j = 0
   while j < numberOfElements
     while i < numberOfElements
       if listOfNames [ i ]
```

```
      endwhile
   endprocedure
```

(d) It has been decided that because of the large number of data items, the bubble sort is too slow and that an insertion sort is going to be used. Explain the basic steps of an insertion sort. **(4 marks)**

....

....

....

....

(Example student responses and mark scheme on p. 183)

2   A football fan has been using a text editor to keep a record of how his favourite team does in each match during a season. The problem with this method is that he is finding it difficult to see how many points they have gained and their goal difference. His friend has said she can write a small program to help him.

(a) The first procedure of the code she is going to write is displayMenu( ) (the main menu interface), which will do the following:
  ➢ Display the options "1. Enter Score", "2. Display Progress" and "3. Exit".
  ➢ Ask which option the user wants and read in that option.
  ➢ Continually repeat the above until option 3 is selected.
  ➢ Within the loop, if option 1 is selected then it calls the procedure enterScore( ), and if option 2 is selected then it calls the procedure teamProgress( ).

Write the pseudocode for the procedure displayMenu( ).   **(7 marks)**

....

....

....

....

(b) The procedure enterScore( ) will write the match score entered to a file (myTeam.dat).
The procedure will:
➢ ask if the match is home or away (input is a single character 'H' or 'A'), and convert input
to uppercase
➢ ask for his team's score – score in range 0 to 9
➢ ask for opposing team's score – score range 0 to 9
➢ combine the three inputs above and write them to a file

For example, H0:2 means his team played at home and lost by 2 goals; A1:2 means his team
played away and won by 1 goal. Note: validation of inputs is required.

Write the pseudocode for the procedure enterScore( ). **(8 marks)**

 OCR GCSE (9–1) Computer Science Exam Question Practice

....

....

....

....

....

....

....

(c) The function teamProgress( ) reads all the records from the team file and displays the total number of points gained (3 for each win, 1 for each draw and 0 for each loss) and the total goal difference (the total number of goals they have scored minus the total number of goals scored against them). For example:

A0:2 they have won, so gain 3 points and the goal difference for this game is +2.

H1:1 they drew, so gain 1 point and the goal difference for this game is +0.

H1:2 they lost, so gain 0 points and the goal difference is –1.

Complete the following pseudocode by filling in the blank spaces. **(8 marks)**

```
procedure teamProgress( )
  teamPoints = 0
  goalDiff = 0
  teamFile = _ _ _ _ _ _ _ _ _ _ _ _ _ _ _ _ _ _ _ ("myTeam.dat")
  while _ _ _ _ _ _ _ _ _ _ _ _ _ _ _ _ _ _ _ _ myFile.endOfFile()
    matchDetails = teamFile.readLine()
    playedWhere = matchDetails. _ _ _ _ _ _ _ _ _ _ _ _ _ _ _ _ _ _ _
    homeScore = _ _ _ _ _ _ _ _ _ _ _ _ _ _ _ _ _ _ _ _
    awayScore = _ _ _ _ _ _ _ _ _ _ _ _ _ _ _ _ _ _ _ _
    if homeScore _ _ _ _ _ _ _ _ _ _ _ _ _ _ _ _ _ _ _ _ awayScore then
      teamPoints = teamPoints + 1
    elseif playedWhere == "H" then
      if homeScore > awayScore then
        teamPoints = teamPoints + 3
        goalDiff = goalDiff + homeScore - awayScore
    else
      goalDiff = goalDiff + homeScore - awayScore
    endif
  elseif _ _ _ _ _ _ _ _ _ _ _ _ _ _ _ _ _ _ _ _ then
    teamPoints = teamPoints + 3
    goalDiff = goalDiff + awayScore - homeScore
  else
    goalDiff = goalDiff + awayScore - homeScore
  endif
    endwhile

    _ _ _ _ _ _ _ _ _ _ _ _ _ _ _ _ _ _ _
    print("Total points is ",teamPoints)
    print("The goal difference is ",goalDiff)
  endprocedure
```

Total: 23 marks

(Example student responses and mark scheme on p. 188)

2.2 Programming techniques

1   (a) When programming, there are three basic constructs that we can use to control the flow of the program. Name, describe and give an example of each.   (9 marks)

....

....

....

....

....

....

....

....

(b) Describe the operation of the following SQL command.
    SELECT firstName,surname FROM studentList
    WHERE candidateNumber > 1500 AND class = '4F';   (4 marks)

....

....

....

....

(c) Write an SQL command that will list all the fields in table studentList for all students in the forms starting with a 4 (i.e. 4F, 4G) or if the surname of the student contains at least one character 'z'.   (4 marks)

....

....

....

....

Total: 17 marks

(Example student responses and mark scheme on p. 193)

2.3 Producing robust programs

1   (a) One of the types of error we find when translating a program is a syntax error. Describe
        what a syntax error is and the likely causes of creating one.   (3 marks)

        ....

        ....

        ....

    (b) Describe a logic error and give an example.   (2 marks)

        ....

        ....

    (c) One type of testing is iterative. Describe iterative testing.   (4 marks)

        ....

        ....

        ....

        ....

Total: 9 marks

(Example student responses and mark scheme on p. 195)

2   As part of a computerised board game, the board is broken up into a grid 15 (x) by 12 (y), with
    the top left grid location being [1,1] and the bottom right being [15,12]. A procedure has been
    written to take in the x and y coordinates and check them to make sure they are valid. If they
    are not valid, an error message is displayed to say 'invalid entry'. If the entry is valid, a message
    to say 'valid entry' is displayed.

    (a) Complete the following test table for the procedure.   (4 marks)

Test data		Type of test	Expected outcome
x	y		
12	10	Valid	Valid entry
		In range	
		Out of range	
		Null	
		Invalid	

(b) Why do we test programs? **(2 marks)**

....

....

Total: 6 marks

(Example student responses and mark scheme on p. 196)

3 **(a)** When entering user input into a program, we often use validation. What is validation and what does it do? **(2 marks)**

....

....

(b) When validating an input, we can use one or more validation techniques such as a length check. Name and give a definition of four other validation techniques. **(8 marks)**

....

....

....

....

....

....

....

....

Total: 10 marks

(Example student responses and mark scheme on p. 197)

2.4 Computational logic

1 **(a)** Explain why data are represented in binary form for a computer system rather than using denary form. **(5 marks)**

....

....

....

....

(b) Complete the following truth table for an OR gate. (2 marks)

A	B	P
FALSE	FALSE	FALSE
FALSE	TRUE	
TRUE	FALSE	TRUE
TRUE	TRUE	

(c) Complete the following truth table for the Boolean statement Q = A AND (NOT B). (4 marks)

A	B	Q
FALSE	FALSE	
FALSE	TRUE	
TRUE	FALSE	
TRUE	TRUE	

(d) Draw the logic circuit for the following truth table. (4 marks)

A	B	C	OUTPUT
FALSE	FALSE	FALSE	FALSE
FALSE	FALSE	TRUE	TRUE
FALSE	TRUE	FALSE	FALSE
FALSE	TRUE	TRUE	TRUE
TRUE	FALSE	FALSE	FALSE
TRUE	FALSE	TRUE	TRUE
TRUE	TRUE	FALSE	TRUE
TRUE	TRUE	TRUE	TRUE

Total: 15 marks

(Example student responses and mark scheme on p. 198)

2 (a) Explain the difference between mathematical operators DIV and MOD.   (4 marks)

....

....

....

....

(b) Evaluate the following formula:
$$14 + 6 * 3 - 2^3 =$$
(1 mark)

....

(c) Explain why we use brackets (parentheses) in mathematical formulas.   (3 marks)

....

....

....

Total: 8 marks

(Example student responses and mark scheme on p. 201)

2.5 Translators and facilities of languages

1   As part of her OCR A-level computing course, Rebecca has to complete a programming project. She has decided that the project will be a maths game for a local primary school.

(a) When choosing the programming language to be used, Rebecca has to decide whether to use a high-level language or a low-level language. Explain the difference between a high-level language and a low-level language and give an example of each.   (5 marks)

....

....

....

....

(b) If Rebecca decides to use a high-level programming language, why will she need a translator?   (2 marks)

....

....

(c) Rebecca decides that she will use a compiler to translate the high-level code. Describe the characteristics of a compiler. **(4 marks)**

....

....

....

....

(d) Besides the compiler and assembler, there is one other type of translator. Name and describe this translator. **(6 marks)**

....

....

....

....

....

....

(e) Rebecca is going to use an integrated development environment (IDE) during the development of her program. Name three common tools or facilities that are available within an IDE. **(3 marks)**

....

....

....

Total: 20 marks

(Example student responses and mark scheme on p. 202)

2.6 Data representation

1   (a) Convert the denary value 65 to binary held in a byte. **(1 mark)**

....

(b) Convert the denary value 47 to a hexadecimal value. **(1 mark)**

....

(c) How many bits are needed to hold a single hexadecimal digit? **(1 mark)**

....

(d) Add together the following two 8-bit binary numbers. Give your response in an 8-bit binary format. **(2 marks)**

0 1 1 0 1 1 0 1
0 1 0 1 1 1 0 1

(e) A check digit is often included as part of a stock number or barcode. What is the purpose of a check digit? **(2 marks)**

....

....

....

(f) ASCII is an example of a character set. Define the term 'character set' and give another example. **(3 marks)**

....

....

....

....

Total: 10 marks

(Example student responses and mark scheme on p. 205)

2   A 14 GB folder containing digital images is to be completely copied on to a single 10 GB memory stick (pen drive) to be posted to a client for printing on poster photographic paper.
(a) How can we fit 14 GB of data on to a 10 GB memory stick? **(2 marks)**

....

....

(b) There are two methods to make an image smaller, one which retains the image quality and another which may reduce the quality slightly. Name both. **(2 marks)**

....

....

(c) The original size of a digital image is 1042 × 1962 pixels. On receiving the memory stick, the client is going to enlarge the image to twice its original size for printing. Which of the two methods to make an image file size smaller would you use and why? **(3 marks)**

....

....

....

Total: 7 marks

(Example student responses and mark scheme on p. 207)

3 Aaliyah is a bird watcher who is going to record bird songs on her old 4 GB tablet, which she will later transfer to her laptop for editing.

(a) The tablet receives the sound from the microphone. Explain how the tablet converts the sound to a file. **(3 marks)**

....

....

....

(b) Aaliyah has found that the storage on her tablet often becomes full before she has had a chance to download the audio files. She decides to reduce the sample rate she records at. What will be the effect of this change? **(4 marks)**

....

....

....

Total: 7 marks

(Example student responses and mark scheme on p. 208)

EXAMPLE RESPONSES AND MARK SCHEMES

The student responses

This section shows sample answers from two students. One set (A) is strong, the other (B) weaker. The answers are followed by expert comments (shown by the icon ⓔ) that indicate where credit is due. In the weaker answers, they also point out areas for improvement, specific problems and common errors.

Component 1 Computer systems

1.1 Systems architecture

Question 1
Student A

(a)   Fetch

Decode

Execute

ⓔ **This is an exact match to the mark scheme. 3 marks**

(b)   Use the Arithmetic Logic Unit (ALU) to calculate complicated mathematical functions.

Move data from one memory location to another.

Jump to different addresses in a program based on decisions that the CPU makes.

ⓔ **Award 1 mark for naming any one of these actions and 1 mark for a full description. 2 marks**

(c)   Address bus – used when the CPU needs to read or write to a memory location. It specifies that memory location on the address bus.

Data bus – sends or receives data from memory to allow every component to communicate with other components.

Control bus – send control signals around the CPU to tell the CPU what to do with the data or memory location it is accessing at that time. This includes reading data from a location or writing data to a location

ⓔ **The three elements are named correctly and expanded clearly. It is nice to see examples used to illustrate the answer in the explanation of the control bus. 6 marks**

Question 1
Student B

(a) Fetch–execute cycle

ⓔ **Two of the three possible responses are named. 2 marks**

(b) ALU to calculate

ⓔ **This student has not described what could be calculated, so gets only 1 mark. 1 mark**

(c) Address bus – sends an address to memory.

Data bus – sends or receives data from memory.

Control bus – send signals to control actions of the CPU.

ⓔ **This answer gives the bare minimum for each point. In the third point the reference to actions shows slightly more understanding but is not sufficient for the second mark. 3 marks**

Question 1 mark scheme

(a) 1 mark for each of the following points:
- fetch
- decode
- execute

Hints and tips
As students are asked to 'State…', the expected response is one word or a simple phrase for each function.

(b) Up to 2 marks for one explanation from:
- Use the ALU… (1)
    - …to calculate mathematical data. (1)

The total of 2 marks is allocated for the fuller expansion.
- To move data… (1)
    - …from one memory location to the CPU, or vice versa. (1)

The total of 2 marks is allocated for the fuller expansion.
- Jumps/goes to different addresses… (1)
    - …based on the value in the accumulator. (1)

The total of 2 marks is allocated for the fuller expansion.

Hints and tips
As students are asked to 'Describe…', the response is expected to be in some detail and therefore a short phrase will not gain maximum marks.

(c) **Address bus**

When the CPU needs to read from or write to memory… (1)

…it specifies that memory location on the address bus. (1)

Data bus

Sends to or receives data from memory… (1)

…to move it to and from the CPU. (1)

Control bus

Carries control signals around the CPU… (1)

…to tell the CPU what to do with the selected data / memory location. (1)

Hints and tips

As students are asked to 'Give…', a response with more than a single word is expected.

Question 2
Student A

(a) Parallel processing is where more than one instruction can be processed at the same time, enabling a significant increase in the performance of the computer. This is because with multiple CPUs it can begin to fetch and decode another set of instructions while it is processing others.

ⓔ An accurate description is communicated well. **3 marks**

(b)

Steps	Explanation
Fetch	It fetches the data and instructions from main memory (i.e. RAM) and stores them into registers
Decode	It decodes and organises the instructions into significant parts
Execute	It executes those individual parts of the instructions

ⓔ These are clear and accurate explanations for each of the three steps. **3 marks**

(c) 4 GHz

ⓔ This is the correct answer. **1 mark**

Question 2
Student B

(a) Parallel processing means it can carry out several instructions at the same time. Rebecca would find the computer quicker.

(e) The description of parallel processing is accurate (1). 'Quicker' on its own is not enough to gain the second mark. However, the student puts their response into context (1). **2 marks**

(b)

Steps	Explanation
Fetch	Fetch instructions from RAM for the registers
Decode	It turns it into a language that humans can understand
Execute	It means that the data is processed

(e) The 'Fetch' explanation is not fluently described, but it gives the important points (1). The response for 'Decode' is inaccurate. The explanation for 'Execute' meets the second criterion for this mark (1). **2 marks**

(c) 4,000,000,000

(e) This student has not given the response in the requested format, so the mark is not awarded.

Question 2 mark scheme

(a) 1 mark for each of the following points:

➤ Parallel processing is when multiple CPUs (or cores)…
➤ …work together, simultaneously processing the same program.
➤ This means that certain programs will execute more quickly than they would with a single processor.

Hints and tips

There are 3 marks available, so look for three pieces of information.

(b) 1 mark for each row completed correctly.

Steps	Explanation
Fetch	It fetches the data and instructions from main memory (i.e. RAM) and stores them into registers
Decode	It decodes and organises the instructions into significant parts/the instruction in the current instruction register (CIR) is interpreted
Execute	It executes those individual parts of the instructions/data processing takes place

(c) The correct answer is 4 GHz.

Question 3
Student A

(a) A MAR can hold two different kinds of addresses. It can store the address of an instruction or it can store the address for data to be fetched from or stored to.

(e) **This answer is accurate and states that it can store either the address of an instruction or the address of data. For the second mark the student has indicated this can be the address to fetch data or an instruction from or the address of the location in which to store data. 2 marks**

(b) An MDR contains the data after they have been fetched from the computer storage. It holds anything copied from RAM ready for the processor to use.

(e) **This is accurate and clearly stated. 2 marks**

(c)

Purpose	MDR or MAR?
CPU register where data to be transferred to or from memory are stored temporarily	MDR
CPU register where the address of a memory location is kept so that data can be written to or read from it	MAR
It is connected to the address bus	MAR
It contains the data/instruction after a fetch from the computer storage	MDR

(e) **The correct response is given for each row. 4 marks**

Question 3
Student B

(a) It stores addresses.

(e) **This is too vague and fails to state what addresses are stored. No marks are awarded.**

(b) It contains data that have been fetched.

(e) **This is accurate but needs to be expanded to gain full marks. 1 mark**

(c)

Purpose	MDR or MAR?
CPU register where data to be transferred to or from memory are stored temporarily	MDR MAR
CPU register where the address of a memory location is kept so that data can be written to or read from it	MAR
It is connected to the address bus	MAR
It contains the data/instruction after a fetch from the computer storage	

(e) **The first response is duplicated, so no mark is awarded. The second and third responses are accurate for 1 mark each, but the final response has been left blank, so no mark is awarded.**
2 marks

Question 3 mark scheme

(a) The MAR holds the address/location…

…to which the CPU is about to read from or write to memory.

(1 mark for address/location and 1 mark for CPU to read/write from/to memory)

(b) 2 marks for any of the following marking points. To gain full marks, the response must contain both parts of the marking point.
- When a piece of data or an instruction is fetched from memory, it is temporarily held in the Memory Data Register/MDR.
- Data is held in the MDR before it is sent to be stored in RAM.
- It contains the data after a fetch from the computer storage and holds anything copied from RAM ready for the processor to use it.

(c) 1 mark for each row completed correctly.

Purpose	MDR or MAR?
CPU register where data to be transferred to or from memory are stored temporarily	MDR
CPU register where the address of a memory location is kept so that data can be written to or read from it	MAR
It is connected to the address bus	MAR
It contains the data/instruction after a fetch from the computer storage	MDR

Question 4
Student A

(a) Memory Address Register

⊕ **This is the correct definition. 1 mark**

(b) An MAR is a CPU register that stores the memory address of data to be fetched or the memory address that data will be sent to and where they will be stored.

⊕ **This is a full and accurate response. 3 marks**

Question 4
Student B

(a) Memory Address Registry

⊕ **The word 'Registry' is incorrect: the word 'Register' must be used. No mark is awarded.**

(b) It has the address in memory of data.

⊕ **This student gives only one piece of information, whereas three pieces are expected. 1 mark**

Question 4 mark scheme

(a) The correct answer is Memory Address Register.

Hints and tips

When a definition is asked for, include in your answer the full words that the initials stand for.

(b) Look for three distinct pieces of information for 1 mark each, for example:
- ⟩ It is a CPU register that stores a memory address.
- ⟩ It stores either the memory address to fetch data from…
- ⟩ …or the memory address where data will be sent to and stored.

Question 5
Student A

(a) A program counter is a register in a CPU.

℮ This is an accurate response. **1 mark**

(b) It contains the address of the next instruction to be executed.

℮ This is also an accurate response. **1 mark**

(c)

Name	Definition
A program	A set of instructions for a computer to perform
An instruction	An order/instruction within the program for the computer processor to carry out
An address	A specific location in memory or storage
A register	A small set of locations to hold data that the processor uses

℮ All the rows are correct. **4 marks**

Question 5
Student B

(a) Register

℮ This response is too vague, so no mark is awarded.

(b) The next instruction

℮ This is not enough, it must say address. No mark awarded.

(c)

Name	Definition
Application	A set of instructions for a computer to perform
Instructions	An order/instruction within the program for the computer processor to carry out
An address	A specific location in memory or storage
Program	A small set of locations to hold data that the processor uses

ℯ The first two rows are acceptable, the third is correct, but the fourth is wrong. **3 marks**

Question 5 mark scheme

(a) Registers

(b) 1 mark for saying that it holds the address of the instruction to be run.

(c) 1 mark for each row completed correctly.

Name	Definition
A program	A set of instructions for a computer to perform
An instruction	An order/instruction within the program for the computer processor to carry out
An address	A specific location in memory or storage
A register	A small set of locations to hold data that the processor uses

Question 6
Student A

(a) The program counter holds the address of the next instruction that is to be fetched-decoded-executed.

ℯ This student gives the correct response, including the required words 'next instruction' and 'fetched-decoded-executed'. **1 mark**

(b) When the first instruction is executed, the program counter will be updated automatically with a new value ready for the next instruction. The next instruction is in memory so it needs to be taken out of memory.

ℯ This student gives a full and accurate response. **4 marks**

Question 6
Student B

(a) It holds the next instruction.

(e) **The response must say the 'address' of the next instruction, so no mark is awarded.**

(b) The program counter is updated and the next instruction is fetched.

(e) **This student's response is accurate as far as it goes, even though the explanations are brief. However, to gain the remaining 2 marks, the student needs to provide a more complete answer. 2 marks**

Question 6 mark scheme

(a) The address of the next instruction that is to be fetched-decoded-executed.

(b) 4 marks from:
- Once the first instruction is fetched, the register is incremented to point at the next instruction…
- …so the program counter is updated…
- …with a new value for the next instruction.
- The next instruction is in memory…
- …so it needs to be taken out of memory, or fetched.
- The process is repeated until the end of the program.

Question 7
Student A

If an accumulator needed to sum up a list of numbers, the accumulator would start by being set at 0 (zero). Then each number, one by one, would be added to the value in the accumulator. The result would only be written back to main memory when all the numbers had been added. If a result had to be sent back to main memory each time one number was added to the next one in the list, then fetched again, a lot of time would be used. Also, the access to main memory is slower than accessing the accumulator.

(e) **This student states that each number in the list is added to the accumulator (1), that only the final value is written back to memory (1) when all the numbers have been added (1), and that if each intermediate total were to be written back to memory and then fetched again, a lot of time would be wasted (2). They also note that access to main memory is slower than access to the accumulator (1). 6 marks**

Question 7
Student B

An accumulator doesn't send a result back to main memory until the final answer is calculated. An accumulator is quicker than main memory.

ⓔ **The first sentence is accurate (1). No marks are awarded for 'an accumulator is quicker than main memory' because it is the access that is quicker and 'access time' is not mentioned. 1 mark**

Question 7 mark scheme

1 mark for each of the following points:
➢ When the ALU performs several calculations, it does not send each intermediate value back to memory.
➢ The accumulator only sends the final value to memory…
➢ …when all the intermediate steps in a calculation have been completed.
➢ If a result had to be sent back to main memory each time one number was added to the next one in the list and then fetched again…
➢ …a lot of time would be used.
➢ Access to main memory is slower than access to the accumulator.

Question 8
Student A

(a) Control Unit, Arithmetic Logic Unit, Registers

ⓔ **All correct. 3 marks**

(b) Logic tests and comparisons.

ⓔ **This is an accurate response. 2 marks**

(c)

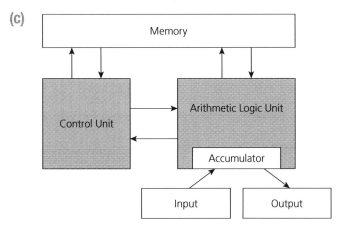

ⓔ **The diagram is labelled correctly. 4 marks**

Question 8
Student B

(a) Control, ALU, Execute

(e) No mark is awarded for the first response because this student needed to state 'Control Unit', not just 'Control'. 'ALU' gains 1 mark. The third point is incorrect. **1 mark**

(b) Adding and multiplying.

(e) This student must say adding and subtracting as well as multiplying and dividing, so no marks are awarded.

(c) Control Unit and Arithmetic Logic Unit. Input.

(e) The responses are written separately to the diagram, but this should not be penalised as the answers are correct and in the right order, enabling 3 marks. No mark is awarded for 'output', which is missing. **3 marks**

Question 8 mark scheme

(a) 1 mark for each of the following points:
   - ▷ Control Unit
   - ▷ Arithmetic Logic Unit/ALU
   - ▷ Registers

Hints and tips

There is 1 mark for each correct response. If you are unsure of a response, it is a good idea to guess one from the list of words given, to give yourself the opportunity to gain an extra mark.

(b) 2 marks from:
   - ▷ Arithmetic operations (1 mark) accept e.g. addition, subtraction, multiplication, division
   - ▷ Logical tests
   - ▷ Comparisons

(c) 1 mark for each of the following points, either inserted into the diagram or written as a list:
   - ▷ Control Unit/CU
   - ▷ Arithmetic Logic Unit/ALU
   - ▷ Input
   - ▷ Output

Question 9
Student A

Memory or RAM holds data and the program that is processing that data/program and data currently in use.

The Control Unit executes instructions from the program and moves the program and data in and out of memory. A register holds values meantime, for example an Accumulator is a register.

Input and output: this is where the user interacts with the computer, passing data to be stored in registers.

Arithmetic Logic Unit or ALU: this is where calculations are carried out, including add, multiply, divide, subtract; comparisons of data can also be made such as > or <.

Bus: information flows between the parts of a computer along the bus. There is also an address bus that identifies different locations in memory/RAM.

ⓔ **This answer is well explained for full marks. 10 marks**

Question 9
Student B

Memory or RAM holds programs and data currently in use.

The Control Unit executes instructions and moves the program and data in and out of memory.

Input and output

Bus: all the information flows between the parts of a computer along the bus.

ⓔ **This is a good explanation of memory/RAM (2) and the Control Unit (2). Input and output are mentioned, but there is no explanation and there is only a partial explanation of a bus (1). There is nothing on the ALU. Nevertheless, it is a good try. 5 marks**

Question 9 mark scheme

Look for 2 distinct marks for each section. Where one section is fully explained, 3 marks may be awarded, but the total marks for this question are 10.

Memory or RAM
▷ Holds data currently in use **and** the program that is processing it.

Control Unit
▷ Executes the instructions given by the program.
▷ Moves the data and the program in and out of memory.
▷ A register holds values meantime/has one or more registers to hold data being operated on/for example an Accumulator is a register.

Input and output
▷ User interacting with the computer.
▷ Values pass in and out…
▷ …while data are stored in registers.
▷ Every following operation is able to read or write to any location in memory.

Arithmetic Logic Unit (ALU)

▷ Calculations are carried out in the ALU/operands and code are used to inform the ALU which operations to carry out on the data input …

▷ …includes add, subtract, multiply, divide.

▷ Data can be compared, such as > (greater than), < (less than), = (equal to).

Bus

▷ The address bus identifies different locations in memory/RAM.

▷ The information flows between the different locations along the bus.

Hints and tips

For computer science, an essay format is not essential. Bullet points, for example, are equally acceptable.

Question 10
Student A

ALU: carries out arithmetic and logical operations.

CU: controls the flow of all data and information and it carries out all of the instructions stored in the program.

Registers: these are temporary storage areas for data or instructions in the processor. They can hold and transfer data and can carry out arithmetic and logic operations quickly.

ⓔ **This is a full and accurate response, gaining 2 marks for each point. 6 marks**

Question 10
Student B

ALU: calculates arithmetic operations.

CU: carries out instructions in a program.

Registers: temporary storage for data or instructions.

ⓔ **This student's responses are accurate as far as they go, but they are incomplete so are awarded 1 mark each. 3 marks**

Question 10 mark scheme

6 marks from:

ALU (1 mark for each of the following points):
▷ Carries out arithmetic and logical operations…

▷ …including addition, subtraction, multiplication and division.

CU (2 marks from):
▷ Controls the flow of all data and information.

▷ It decodes instructions.

▷ Manages the execution of instructions by fetching instructions from memory.

Registers (2 marks from):

≫ Temporary storage for instructions or data/hold and transfer data or instructions.

≫ Perform arithmetic or logical comparisons…

≫ …faster than main memory.

Question 11
Student A

	ALU	CU	MAR	MDR
It carries out arithmetic and logic comparison functions	✓			
It makes decisions and sends the appropriate signal to other parts of the computer		✓		
It provides a temporary memory storage location within the processor			✓	
It carries out all the calculations and makes decisions on the data sent to the processor	✓			
It controls the timing of operations in the computer and controls the instructions sent to the processor and the peripheral devices		✓		
It manages all of the computer's resources		✓		
It holds the address of the cell to be fetched or stored			✓	
It holds the data value being fetched or stored				✓

ⓔ This student has read the statements carefully and gives the correct response in each case. **8 marks**

Question 11
Student B

	ALU	CU	MAR	MDR
It carries out arithmetic and logic comparison functions	✓			
It makes decisions and sends the appropriate signal to other parts of the computer				✓
It provides a temporary memory storage location within the processor				✓
It carries out all the calculations and makes decisions on the data sent to the processor	✓			
It controls the timing of operations in the computer and controls the instructions sent to the processor and the peripheral devices		✓		
It manages all of the computer's resources		✓		
It holds the address of the cell to be fetched or stored	✓	✓	✓	✓
It holds the data value being fetched or stored				✓

ⓔ The second row is indicated as MDR; it should have been CU as it is the Control Unit that makes the decisions and sends the appropriate signal to other parts of the computer, so no mark is awarded. The penultimate row has been ticked multiple times, so no mark is awarded. **6 marks**

Question 11 mark scheme

1 mark for each row completed correctly.

	ALU	CU	MAR	MDR
It carries out arithmetic and logic comparison functions	✓			
It makes decisions and sends the appropriate signal to other parts of the computer		✓		
It provides a temporary memory storage location within the processor			✓	✓
It carries out all the calculations and makes decisions on the data sent to the processor	✓			
It controls the timing of operations in the computer and controls the instructions sent to the processor and the peripheral devices		✓		
It manages all of the computer's resources		✓		
It holds the address of the cell to be fetched or stored			✓	
It holds the data value being fetched or stored				✓

Hints and tips

Read and consider each statement carefully before inserting your tick for each one.

Question 12
Student A

(a)

G	The CPU sends a signal to all other hardware so the instruction is then executed
C	The stored instruction is fetched from this address
A	The CPU has to get the first instruction in the program
E	The instruction passes back to the CPU on the data bus
F	The instruction is decoded by the CPU
D	The instruction is fetched by putting it on the data bus
B	The address of the instruction it wants to fetch is put on the address bus

ⓔ All the rows are correct. **6 marks**

(b) Register

ⓔ Correct. **1 mark**

Question 12
Student B

(a)

B	The CPU sends a signal to all other hardware so the instruction is then executed
C	The stored instruction is fetched from this address
A	The CPU has to get the first instruction in the program
D	The instruction passes back to the CPU on the data bus
E	The instruction is decoded by the CPU
F	The instruction is fetched by putting it on the data bus
G	The address of the instruction it wants to fetch is put on the address bus

ⓔ Only row C is correct. It appears that the student did not have the knowledge to answer this question correctly, so they attempted to put the response into alphabetical order where C just happened to fall in the correct place. **1 mark**

(b) It is the computer's register.

ⓔ Although the word 'register' is included in this response, the context in which it is written renders the response inaccurate. No mark is awarded.

Question 12 mark scheme

(a) No mark is awarded for row A as it is given in the question. 1 mark for each of the other rows completed correctly.

G	The CPU sends a signal to all other hardware so the instruction is then executed
C	The stored instruction is fetched from this address
A	The CPU has to get the first instruction in the program
E	The instruction passes back to the CPU on the data bus
F	The instruction is decoded by the CPU
D	The instruction is fetched by putting it on the data bus
B	The address of the instruction it wants to fetch is put on the address bus

Hints and tips

You are required to mark each statement with a letter indicating the order of the actions. The first one, A, is given already. What you need to do now is to look for where the B is to go, in order to show the action that occurs after A.

(b) The correct answer is 'register'.

Question 13
Student A

Component	Definition
Arithmetic Logic Unit	Carries out/performs mathematical operations and any logic comparisons
Memory Address Register	The address in main memory currently being read or written
Control Unit	It decodes the instruction given by the program
Program counter	This is incremental, meaning that it keeps track of memory addresses needed for the instruction to be executed next

ℯ All the rows are correct. **4 marks**

Question 13
Student B

Component	Definition
Arithmetic Logic Unit	Carries out/performs mathematical operations and any logic comparisons
Memory Address Register	The address in main memory currently being read or written
Control Unit	It decodes the instruction given by the program
Control Unit	This is incremental, meaning that it keeps track of memory addresses needed for the instruction to be executed next

ℯ The fourth row is incorrect; it is the program counter that is incremental. **3 marks**

Question 13 mark scheme

1 mark for each row completed correctly.

Component	Definition
Arithmetic Logic Unit	Carries out/performs mathematical operations and any logic comparisons
Memory Address Register	The address in main memory currently being read or written
Control Unit	It decodes the instruction given by the program
Program counter	This is incremental, meaning that it keeps track of memory addresses needed for the instruction to be executed next

Question 14
Student A

(a) Cache size, clock speed, number of cores

🄴 This is a full response. **3 marks**

(b) A bigger cache can store more instructions, therefore saving time if the next instruction is already present in the cache.
The clock speed decides the rate at which instructions are carried out so if the clock ticks quicker, instructions are carried out quicker.
A core fetches and decodes instructions so if there are more cores, instructions can be fetched and decoded quicker.

🄴 Two points for each characteristic listed correctly. **6 marks**

Question 14
Student B

(a) Size
Speed
Number of cores

🄴 This response is too vague; there is no indication of what the size or the speed relates to. The third item, 'Number of cores', is correct. **1 mark**

(b) Because the cache is closer to the CPU than main memory, there is less distance to travel – saves time. If the clock ticks faster the CPU runs more quickly. A higher number of cores means that instructions are done more quickly.

🄴 This student gives one point for each characteristic, but two points are required. **3 marks**

Question 14 mark scheme

(a) 1 mark for each of the following points:
  ▷ cache size
  ▷ clock speed
  ▷ number of cores

(b) Any 2 marking points from each section to make 6 marks.

Cache size
  ▷ The CPU cache is between the processor and main memory, so data do not have to travel far.
  ▷ A bigger cache can store more instructions.
  ▷ A bigger cache makes it more likely that the next instruction is in the cache already…
  ▷ …therefore a bigger cache size can improve the performance of the CPU.

Clock speed
  ▷ Clock speed determines how quickly an instruction can be carried out.
  ▷ Instructions are fetched and executed more quickly when there is a faster clock speed.

> Each operation uses a fixed number of ticks…
> …so if the clock ticks faster, more instructions can be processed.

Number of cores
> A core fetches and decodes instructions.
> More cores means that instructions can be fetched and decoded at the same time…
> …because the tasks are split between the cores, multi-tasking is enabled.

Hints and tips

There are 6 marks available for this question, so try to find six different things to say.

Question 15
Student A

(a) Mobile phone networks
WiFi routers

ⓔ Both responses are correct. **2 marks**

(b) Firmware

ⓔ This is the correct response. **1 mark**

(c) For medical applications where an insulin pump is controlled by an embedded system, it must be completely reliable and accurate or the patient may receive too much, or not enough, medication.
In transportation there is an embedded system that controls anti-lock brakes and if the system were not totally reliable then car crashes might occur, resulting in injury and death.
In industry where robotics are used, if the embedded system fails this could lead to many problems such as injury to workers.

ⓔ Three appropriate examples, with reasons, each gain 2 marks. **6 marks**

Question 15
Student B

(a) Mobile phones
Telephones

ⓔ Mobile phones is correct, but the second answer should be 'telephone networks'. **1 mark**

(b) Operating system

ⓔ This is incorrect. Firmware is the name of the type of program written for an embedded system. No mark is awarded.

(c) In cars lots of things are controlled with embedded systems and any system that didn't work properly like a fuel injection system may put lives in danger.
It controls aircraft.

ⓔ The first example (transport) and the reason given are accurate. The second example is too vague and there is no reason given. **2 marks**

Question 15 mark scheme

(a) 2 marks from:
  ➢ mobile phone network/mobile phones/cell phones
  ➢ WiFi router
  ➢ telephone networks
  ➢ switches for telephone networks

Or any other reasonable answer.

(b) The correct answer is firmware.

(c) 2 marks for each example and the reason given. For example:
  ➢ Transport: for anti-brake systems in cars. If brakes do not perform correctly, there is the possibility of car crashes (or any other reasonable example).
  ➢ Medical: for blood pressure readers so doctors can have accurate data before prescribing treatment/automated control of dosage of drugs (or any reasonable example).
  ➢ Avionics: controlling aircraft where lives could be put in danger if the embedded system failed (or any reasonable example).

Or any other reasonable example with an explanation.

Question 16
Student A

(a) Microwave
Dishwasher
Television

ⓔ **All three examples are correct. 3 marks**

(b) A lot of time and effort goes into developing embedded systems. This means that it takes a long time before the systems can be marketed and even then they may not be absolutely reliable. Once they have been developed, it is quite difficult to change them as they are sometimes limited by the hardware that they have to be able to work with. On the other hand, they are good for the environment as there is a relatively low consumption of power and, once on the market, they become a low-cost item as they may often be bought in bulk by the manufacturers that use them.

ⓔ **Five valid disadvantages and two valid advantages are described. This is a good example of a discussion, but more points could have been made. 7 marks**

Question 16
Student B

(a) Microwave
Washing machine
Cooker

ⓔ **The first two examples each gain 1 mark. The third response is not specific enough, so no mark is awarded. 2 marks**

Question 16 mark scheme

(a) 3 marks from:

>> microwave cooker
>> washing machine
>> dishwasher
>> tumble dryer
>> television
>> digital camera
>> MP3 player

Or any other reasonable response.

(b) 10 marks taken from mention of items such as those listed below. Each advantage or disadvantage should be clearly explained.

Advantages
>> Easily customisable
>> Low power consumption
>> Low cost
>> Enhanced performance

Disadvantages
>> High development efforts
>> Longer time to market
>> Might not be wholly reliable
>> Limitation of hardware

1.2 Memory

Question 1
Student A

(a) Random Access Memory and Read-Only Memory

e Two completely accurate definitions. **2 marks**

(b)

	RAM	ROM
Memory available for the operating system and programs to use when the computer is running	✓	
Memory that holds instructions for booting-up the computer		✓
Memory that requires the computer to be on in order to retain data	✓	
Data are not permanently written to this type of memory	✓	
It is a type of volatile memory	✓	
Data in this type of memory are permanently written		✓
Data in this type of memory are not lost when the computer is switched off		✓
Data in this type of memory are pre-written and come with a computer		✓

(e) **All the rows are correct. 8 marks**

(c) On the motherboard inside the computer.

(e) **This response is correct; it also amplifies the one-word response that would also have gained the mark. 1 mark**

Question 1
Student B

(a) Random Access Memory

(e) **Only one of the two questions is addressed, but the definition is accurate. 1 mark**

(b)

	RAM	ROM
Memory available for the operating system and programs to use when the computer is running	✓	✓
Memory that holds instructions for booting-up the computer		✓
Memory that requires the computer to be on in order to retain data	✓	
Data are not permanently written to this type of memory	✓	
It is a type of volatile memory		✓
Data in this type of memory are permanently written		✓
Data in this type of memory are not lost when the computer is switched off		✓
Data in this type of memory are pre-written and come with a computer	✓	

(e) **The first row loses the mark because both columns are ticked. The fifth and eighth rows are incorrect. 5 marks**

(c) Next to the motherboard.

(e) **The ROM chip is located on the motherboard, not next to it. No mark is awarded.**

Question 1 mark scheme

(a)   1 mark for each of the following points:
  ➢ Random Access Memory
  ➢ Read-Only Memory

Hints and tips

Both definitions must be exactly correct for both marks.

(b)   1 mark for each row completed correctly.

	RAM	ROM
Memory available for the operating system and programs to use when the computer is running	✓	
Memory that holds instructions for booting-up the computer		✓
Memory that requires the computer to be on in order to retain data	✓	
Data are not permanently written to this type of memory	✓	
It is a type of volatile memory	✓	
Data in this type of memory are permanently written		✓
Data in this type of memory are not lost when the computer is switched off		✓
Data in this type of memory are pre-written and come with a computer		✓

Hints and tips

Ticks in both boxes gain no marks.

(c)   The correct answer is motherboard.

Hints and tips

There is only 1 mark available, so a one-word response is acceptable.

Question 2
Student A

(a)   Basic Input Output System

ⓔ **This is the correct definition of the acronym. 1 mark**

(b)   Power-on self-test
       Check RAM installed
       Check if video card installed

ⓔ **Three valid responses. 3 marks**

Question 2
Student B

(a) Basic Input Output Series

(e) **The definition is incorrect. It must be exactly correct to gain the mark, so no mark is awarded.**

(b) Check the amount of RAM
Check type of boot-up
Look for operating system

(e) **The first two responses are correct, but the third is incorrect: 'Look for operating system' is not a check. 2 marks**

Question 2 mark scheme

(a) Basic Input Output System

(b) 3 marks from:
- Power-on self-test/POST.
- Check the type of hard disk installed/check hardware devices/check if video card operational.
- Check the amount of RAM installed.
- Check the type of CPU being used.
- Check if it is a cold boot or a re-boot.
- Check ports.

Hints and tips

There are 3 marks, so make sure that you list three separate checks.

Question 3
Student A

When you turn on your computer, the BIOS carries out its usual sequence, which is something like:
- Checks the CMOS setup for custom settings.
- Loads the interrupt handlers and device drivers.
- Initialises of the registers/power management.
- Performs the power-on self-test (POST).
- Displays the system settings.
- Determines which devices are bootable.
- Initiates the bootstrap sequence.

The ROM BIOS stores the first instruction to be run: the power-on self-test (POST). It checks the BIOS chip, then it tests CMOS RAM. If the POST doesn't detect any battery failure, it continues to initialise the CPU.

ROM is non-volatile, so when the computer is switched off the ROM data are not erased when they are stored permanently.

Non-volatile memory is needed because the computer has to be able to get instructions from the BIOS when it is switched on and it must know some basic things about the hardware in the machine. These basic things can be called its configuration settings.

ⓔ **This is a thorough response with amplifications, so each paragraph gains 2 marks. 8 marks**

Question 3
Student B

The BIOS carries out the boot-up sequence.
Checks are carried out.
ROM is non-volatile meaning it doesn't lose its data when the power is off.

ⓔ **The first two points are too vague to get 2 marks each, so only 1 mark each is awarded. The last point merits only 1 mark because only one piece of information is given. It could have gone on to state why that type of memory is necessary. 3 marks**

Question 3 mark scheme

For 8 marks there should be clear identification and explanation of four different points such as those given below:

▷ POST
▷ boot-up/start-up/power-on
▷ checks
▷ finds operating system
▷ ROM/firmware as used in device other than personal computer system
▷ why it is read-only/non-volatile
▷ BIOS (and what it does)

Hints and tips

There are 8 marks, so make sure you identify and explain at least four different points.

Question 4
Student A

(a) Data being used by the computer

ⓔ **This student correctly answers this basic question. 1 mark**

(b) Because the programs and data files are kept on the hard drive, the processor copies the spreadsheet program from the hard drive into the RAM to be used short-term while the data file is being edited. The data file is saved back to the storage drive after the edits have been made and the spreadsheet program is closed. It is no longer held in RAM now the edits have been completed.

ⓔ **Four points are made correctly. 4 marks**

Question 4
Student B

(a) Data

ⓔ **Data is not enough, there must be reference to currently being used. No mark is awarded.**

(b) You open the spreadsheet software, then the data file. The data are held in RAM while you make the edits, save and close.

ⓔ **1 mark is given for the spreadsheet software and data file being held in RAM. It does not say any more about what happens in RAM. 1 mark**

Question 4 mark scheme

(a) The programs and data currently in use.

(b) An account of the fetch-execute cycle is *not* expected here. Look for four separate steps (1 mark each):
  ≫ The system's processor brings a copy of the spreadsheet program and the file from the storage drive to the RAM for short-term access and use.
  ≫ The processor accesses data from the RAM.
  ≫ Edits are carried out and saved to the storage drive.
  ≫ The program is closed and it, along with the data for the file, is removed from RAM.

Question 5
Student A

Statement	Correct?
RAM provides a workspace to store information that the processor is using	✓
Sometimes a portion of the hard drive is used as extra RAM space	✓
Hard drives are slower than RAM at transferring data	✓
RAM stands for Rapid Access Memory	
DRAM is the most common form of RAM	✓

e This student has ticked the four correct statements. **4 marks**

Question 5
Student B

Statement	Correct?
RAM provides a workspace to store information that the processor is using	✓
Sometimes a portion of the hard drive is used as extra RAM space	✓
Hard drives are slower than RAM at transferring data	
RAM stands for Rapid Access Memory	
DRAM is the most common form of RAM	

e This student has only indicated that two of the four statements are correct. **2 marks**

Question 5 mark scheme

1 mark for each row completed correctly.

Statement	Correct?
RAM provides a workspace to store information that the processor is using	✓
Sometimes a portion of the hard drive is used as extra RAM space	✓
Hard drives are slower than RAM at transferring data	✓
RAM stands for Rapid Access Memory	
DRAM is the most common form of RAM	✓

Question 6
Student A

(a) You need RAM and a hard drive so that the swapping can take place.

e **This student provides a full response. 1 mark**

(b) The process of swapping is the when the operating system moves data between RAM and virtual memory. It does this for the processes that are not needed immediately. It takes them out of the RAM and stores them in virtual memory. When the processes are needed again, it copies the data back to RAM.

e **This shows a good understanding of the process, gaining 1 mark each for the first two sentences and 2 marks each for the last two sentences. 6 marks**

(c) It would be necessary if there is not enough RAM to run a program. Then virtual memory combines the computer's RAM with temporary space on the hard disk, freeing up more space in RAM. Virtual memory helps when RAM is low, as it can move data from the RAM to a paging file.

e **All the points made are correct. The student has also evidenced good understanding in the way this response is expressed. 6 marks**

Question 6
Student B

(a) RAM and cache.

e **This student has the idea of needing RAM, but has incorrectly given cache instead of hard disk drive. No mark is awarded.**

(b) Swapping means taking some data not needed at the moment from RAM into the virtual memory and back again when it is needed.

e **Three points are made, but the process is not fully explained. 3 marks**

(c) Not enough RAM makes it necessary to use virtual memory on the hard disk.

e **This student mentions 'Not enough RAM' (1) and 'necessary to use virtual memory' (1), and also implies that the virtual memory is on the hard disk (within the context of this response) (1). 3 marks**

Question 6 mark scheme

(a) RAM and a hard disk drive.

(b) 1 mark for each of the following points:
  - When the operating system moves data between RAM and virtual memory, the process is called swapping or paging
  - If some processes are not needed straight away, the operating system will move that data…
  - …from the RAM…
  - …to store them in virtual memory on the hard disk.

⤜ The operating system copies the data back into RAM…

⤜ …when it is needed.

(c) Allow 2 marks for each marking point – 1 mark for each half. There should be an action and a corresponding reason for any 2 marks (to max. 6).

⤜ Not enough RAM…needed to run a program or operation.

⤜ In order to free up more RAM, virtual memory can combine the computer's RAM with temporary space on the hard disk.

⤜ If space on RAM becomes low…virtual memory moves data from RAM to a paging file.

⤜ The more RAM a computer has…the faster your programs could run.

Hints and tips

Try to write an action and qualify it with a reason for each pair of marks.

Question 7
Student A

	Correct	Incorrect
Using virtual memory makes the computer run more quickly		✓
Virtual memory is a technique that only uses hardware		✓
Virtual memory is a technique that uses both hardware and software	✓	
Copying to a hard disk takes longer than reading and writing to and from RAM	✓	

ℯ **Each tick is correctly inserted to show the correct and incorrect statements. 4 marks**

Question 7
Student B

	Correct	Incorrect
Using virtual memory makes the computer run more quickly		✓
Virtual memory is a technique that only uses hardware	✓	
Virtual memory is a technique that uses both hardware and software	✓	✓
Copying to a hard disk takes longer than reading and writing to and from RAM	✓	

ℯ **The second statement is incorrect and the third statement has been ticked twice. 2 marks**

Question 7 mark scheme

1 mark for each row completed correctly.

	Correct	Incorrect
Using virtual memory makes the computer run more quickly		✓
Virtual memory is a technique that only uses hardware		✓
Virtual memory is a technique that uses both hardware and software	✓	
Copying to a hard disk takes longer than reading and writing to and from RAM	✓	

Hints and tips

Make sure you tick only one of the boxes against each statement.

Question 8
Student A

(a) Non-volatile
Solid-state
Storage medium
Rewritable

ⓔ **These are the four correct items. 4 marks**

(b) Mobile phones
Memory cards for digital cameras
SSD
Video games hardware

ⓔ **The four examples are correct. 4 marks**

Question 8
Student B

(a) Non-volatile
Storage medium
Rewritable

ⓔ **Although only three responses are given instead of four, they are correct. This student could be encouraged to offer the required number of responses to give them the opportunity of gaining the fourth mark. 3 marks**

(b) Digital audio players
Mobiles
Memory cards for digital cameras

ⓔ **The term 'mobiles' on its own is insufficient, so no mark is awarded for it. 2 marks**

Question 8 mark scheme

(a)   1 mark for each of the following points:
  ▷ Non-volatile
  ▷ Solid-state
  ▷ Storage medium
  ▷ Rewritable

Hints and tips

You could take a tip from how many marks there are to know how many items should be chosen.

(b)   4 marks from:
  ▷ Digital audio players
  ▷ Mobile phones
  ▷ Memory cards for digital cameras
  ▷ Main internal storage for tablet computers/(SSD)
  ▷ Video games hardware

  Or any other reasonable response.

1.3 Storage

Question 1
Student A

(a)   For the long-term storage of photographs. It provides additional storage for data or programs when the computer is turned off.

ⓔ   **Two valid reasons are given together with appropriate examples. 4 marks**

(b)   Magnetic, optical and solid-state.

ⓔ   **All three types given are correct. 3 marks**

(c)

	Optical	Solid state	Magnetic
Blu-ray disk	✓		
Hard disk			✓
CD	✓		
Tablet PC		✓	
Mobile phone		✓	
DVD	✓		
Camera memory card		✓	
Tablet		✓	

ⓔ   **All answers are correct. 8 marks**

Question 1
Student B

(a) Photographs and documents can be kept there.
Delete them easily.
To take files, say, from school to home.

(e) **The first response is an example only, with no reason (1). In the second response, we do not know what 'them' is, so no mark is awarded. In the third response, the student gives a valid example (1). 2 marks**

(b) Magnetic, optic, solid-state.

(e) **'Optic' is incorrect, so no mark is awarded. 2 marks**

(c)

	Optical	Solid state	Magnetic
Blu-ray disk			✓
Hard disk			✓
CD	✓		
Tablet PC			
Mobile phone		✓	
DVD	✓		
Camera memory card		✓	
Tablet		✓	✓

(e) **This student loses 3 marks because 'Blu-ray disk' should be optical, there is no tick for 'Tablet PC' and 'Tablet' is ticked twice. 5 marks**

Question 1 mark scheme

(a) 1 mark for the reason, 1 mark for an appropriate example(s). For example:
  ▷ Long-term storage/back up.
  ▷ Examples: photographs, films, documents.
  ▷ Transferring data between devices.
  ▷ Moving work between home and school.
  ▷ Provides permanent storage.
  ▷ Examples: for data and programs when power off.

(b) 1 mark for each of the following points:
  ▷ Magnetic
  ▷ Optical
  ▷ Solid-state

(c) 1 mark for each row completed correctly.

	Optical	Solid state	Magnetic
Blu-ray disk	✓		
Hard disk			✓
CD	✓		
Tablet PC		✓	
Mobile phone		✓	
DVD	✓		
Camera memory card		✓	
Tablet		✓	

Hints and tips

Tick only one box in each row.

Question 2
Student A

Size	Binary power	Equal to	Common abbreviation
8 bits		1 byte	B
1024 bytes	2^{10}	1 kilobyte	kB
1024 kilobytes	**2^{20}**	1 megabyte	**MB**
1024 megabytes	2^{30}	1 gigabyte	GB
1024 gigabytes	2^{40}	1 terabyte	TB
1024 terabytes	**2^{50}**	1 petabyte	**PB**
1024 petabytes	2^{60}	**1 exabyte**	EB
1024 exabytes	2^{70}	1 zettabyte	ZB
1024 zettabytes	2^{80}	1 yottabyte	YB

ℯ **Each cell has been completed correctly. 6 marks**

Question 2
Student B

Size	Binary power	Equal to	Common abbreviation
8 bits		1 byte	B
1024 bytes	2^{10}	1 kilobyte	kB
1024 kilobytes	**2^{20}**	1 megabyte	**MB**
1024 megabytes	2^{30}	1 gigabyte	GB
1024 gigabytes	2^{40}	1 terabyte	TB
1024 terabytes	**2^{50}**	1 petabyte	
1024 petabytes	2^{60}	**1**	EB
1024	2^{70}	1 zettabyte	ZB
1024 zettabytes	2^{80}	1 yottabyte	YB

ⓔ The answer in the first column is incomplete, so no mark is awarded. Both answers in column 2 are correct for 2 marks. The third column is incomplete, so no mark is awarded. MB is correct for 1 mark; the last blank cell loses a mark. **3 marks**

Question 2 mark scheme

1 mark for each blank cell completed correctly.

Size	Binary power	Equal to	Common abbreviation
8 bits		1 byte	B
1024 bytes	2^{10}	1 kilobyte	kB
1024 kilobytes	**2^{20}**	1 megabyte	**MB**
1024 megabytes	2^{30}	1 gigabyte	GB
1024 gigabytes	2^{40}	1 terabyte	TB
1024 terabytes	**2^{50}**	1 petabyte	**PB**
1024 petabytes	2^{60}	**1 exabyte**	EB
1024 exabytes	2^{70}	1 zettabyte	ZB
1024 zettabytes	2^{80}	1 yottabyte	YB

Question 3
Student A

	Advantages	Disadvantages
Solid-state	No moving parts so cannot damage easily	Vulnerable to magnets or electrical currents
	Produce low heat so could be good for laptops that overheat	Use more power than a hard drive so could make laptop batteries run down more quickly
Magnetic	High capacity	Slow write speed
	External hard drives are easily portable	Not easily portable for fixed hard drives
Optical	Portable	Gets scratched easily
	Can hold a lot of data	Slower than a hard drive

(e) The second advantage for magnetic is allowed as external hard drives are available and are easily portable, even though this advantage is not specified in the mark scheme. **12 marks**

Question 3
Student B

	Advantages	Disadvantages
Solid-state	No moving parts so cannot damage easily	
	Produce low heat so could be good for laptops that overheat	Use more power than a hard drive so could make laptop batteries run down more quickly
Magnetic	High capacity	Slow write speed
Optical	Portable	Gets scratched easily
	Might get damaged easily	Slower than a hard drive

(e) This student gives a disadvantage instead of an advantage for the second response to optical. **7 marks**

Question 3 mark scheme

4 marks for any 2 points from each type. Allow appropriate/reasonable responses.

Solid-state
▷ Advantages: shock resistant/robust/no moving parts to break, easily portable, fast read/write times, easily updated, produce less heat so good for laptops which can overheat, consume less power than mechanical storage devices.
▷ Disadvantages: more expensive the higher capacity of storage needed.

Magnetic

- Advantages: high capacity, relatively inexpensive for amount of space, data can be read from anywhere on hard disk directly.
- Disadvantages: slow write speed, could easily get wiped or altered by magnetic fields etc., not easily portable if fixed inside the computer.

Optical

- Advantages: portable, Blu-ray disks can hold a lot of data, there is usually an optical drive available with a PC, DVDs can hold very large files.
- Disadvantages: can get scratched/damaged easily, slower to access than a hard disk.

Question 4
Student A

(a) Capacity
Speed
Durability
Portability
Reliability
Cost

Six correct considerations are listed. 6 marks

(b) The memory stick is easier to carry around than the portable hard drive (PHD), but they are both quite portable. The PHD would probably hold more than the memory stick, but it would cost more in the first place as PHDs are more expensive to buy than memory sticks. The memory stick is stronger because it is solid-state technology with no moving parts, so it would be more robust than the PHD. Data access is quite fast for a PHD, but it would be even faster if I used a memory stick. I would choose a memory stick.

All points are covered. 10 marks

Question 4
Student B

(a) How much it will hold.
What its download and upload speeds are.
Will it break soon.
How expensive it is.

In the order written, these correspond to: capacity, speed, durability and cost. 4 marks

(b) They are both fairly easy to carry around, but the memory stick is smaller and might fit into my pocket. I could get more on a portable hard drive, but it would be more expensive than buying a memory stick. The memory stick is more robust and faster.

This student states that they are both fairly easy to carry around (1), that the memory stick is smaller/will fit into a pocket (1) and that the portable hard drive is more expensive (1). Only 1 mark is given for 'the memory stick is more robust and faster' because it is not a true comparison as they should say faster than what. 4 marks

Question 4 mark scheme

(a) 1 mark for each of the following points:
- capacity
- speed
- durability
- portability
- reliability
- cost

(b) The following table provides an overview of the type of points that should be mentioned for 1 mark each.

Device	Storage capacity	Data	How portable is it?	Is it robust/ reliable?	Cost
Portable hard drive	Very large	Fast	Average	Robust	Expensive
Memory stick/pen drive	Large	Very fast	Highly portable	Very robust	Medium

Question 5
Student A

(a) The data are stored on the storage medium, but they get there by using the storage device that can read data from the storage medium.

🅮 **This is explained well, evidencing knowledge. 2 marks**

(b)

Capacity	How much data it can store
Speed	This refers to access speed
Durability	How long it will last
Reliability	If it will be reliable over time
Cost	How much it costs to buy in the first place
Portability	Ease of carrying around

🅮 **Although the wording is different from the mark scheme, all the points are covered. 6 marks**

(c) (i) Magnetic tapes

　　(ii) Serial storage

🅮 **Correct responses are given for both parts. 2 marks**

Question 5
Student B

(a) The data are on the storage medium, but they need a device to put them there.

(e) **This student correctly states that the data are on the storage medium (1), but they don't state that the device is a 'storage' device. 1 mark**

(b)

Capacity	How much data can it store?
Speed	How fast is it?
Durability	Will it last a long time?
Reliability	Will it be reliable over time?
Cost	How much does it cost to buy in the first place?
Portability	How easy is it to transport around if necessary?

(e) **The student loses a mark because 'How fast is it?' is not enough; they need to refer to access speed. 5 marks**

(c) (i) Tapes

(ii) Serial

(e) **A mark is awarded for part (ii), but the student needs to say magnetic tapes for part (i). 1 mark**

Question 5 mark scheme

(a) 1 mark for each of the following points:
> The data are stored on the storage medium.
> The device that saves the data to the storage medium/reads data from it is the storage device.

(b) 1 mark for each row completed correctly.

Capacity	How much data it can store
Speed	Access speed
Durability	How robust it is (i.e. does it damage easily?)
Reliability	If it will be reliable over time
Cost	How much it costs to buy in the first place (per GB)
Portability	How easy it is to transport if necessary

(c) 1 mark for each of the following points:
(i) Magnetic tapes (allow sensible alternative).
(ii) Serial storage (allow sensible alternative).

1.4 Wired and wireless networks

Question 1
Student A

(a) (i) Local Area Network

(ii) Wide Area Network

(iii) Wireless Local Area Network

ⓔ **All parts are correct. 3 marks**

(b) WAN: made up of two or more LANs which may be situated anywhere around most of the world.

LAN: computers close to each other that are networked together like in a school.

WLAN: like a LAN, it covers short distances but is connected wirelessly without cables.

ⓔ **This is a good response, which gets full marks. 6 marks**

Question 1
Student B

(a) (i) Local Area Network

(ii) Wide Area Network

(iii) Wireless Network

ⓔ **Part (iii) is incorrect. 2 marks**

(b) WAN: connects LANs together across a distance.

WLAN: connected with no cables but only over short distances.

ⓔ **Although this student's response is brief/concise, it does meet the criteria in the marking points for WAN and WLAN. There is no response for LAN, so a mark is lost. 5 marks**

Question 1 mark scheme

(a) 1 mark for each of the following points:

(i) Local Area Network

(ii) Wide Area Network

(iii) Wireless Local Area Network

(b) 2 marks max. for each section.

WAN

▷ Wide area network covers a large geographical area.

▷ Often made up of two or more LANs.

▷ Often uses third-party communications channels.

LAN
≫ A group of computers in close proximity that are networked together.
≫ Typically in an office, for a home network or in a school or college.
≫ Allows sharing of peripherals and files.

WLAN
≫ (Similar to a LAN as) it covers short distances.
≫ Unlike WAN and LAN, WLAN connects wirelessly instead of through traditional network cabling.
≫ Uses infrared or radio signals to connect.

Question 2
Student A

Either a LAN or a WLAN would be suitable at the moment as there is only one shop and the computers are close together. When they open another shop, another LAN could be set up, then the two LANs could be connected together into a WAN so that the shops could share files such as databases or stock records. A WLAN would be ideal within the shop to allow portability of devices around the shop but these could eventually be connected to a WAN to share data between the shops. I advise a LAN for now, then expand into a WAN once they have more shops.

ℯ **The differences are described correctly and the most suitable type of network is recommended. 5 marks**

Question 2
Student B

A LAN or a WLAN would be best with the one shop, but if they open another shop they could set up a WAN to connect the LANs in both shops. A WLAN wouldn't be suitable for two shops in different towns.

ℯ **This student makes three good points, but there is no final recommendation. 3 marks**

Question 2 mark scheme

4 marks from:
≫ Either a LAN or a WLAN would be suitable for one shop…
≫ …as the computers are close together.
≫ WAN to join the LANs together if they open other shops.
≫ Files can be shared across LAN or WAN.
≫ A WLAN may be used within each shop…
≫ …as will allow portability of devices around the shop.

1 mark for a recommendation: either a LAN or a WLAN for one shop and/or a WAN for when they have more than one shop.

Question 3
Student A

(a) Bandwidth

e **This response is briefly stated but correct. 1 mark**

(b) Downloading has more because more people do more downloading than uploading.

e **This is correct. 2 marks**

(c) Some telephone lines along the route may be older than others and therefore the speed may vary. If the telephone exchange is too far away from a modem, it affects the speed that the data can be transferred.

e **This is a thorough explanation. 4 marks**

Question 3
Student B

(a) The size of the server.

e **This is incorrect, so no mark is awarded.**

(b) Downloading

e **This is enough for 1 mark, but no reason is given. 1 mark**

(c) The quality of phone lines can be different. The exchange is too far away.

e **It is the quality of the signal, not the quality of the phone lines, that can be different. The student does not state what the telephone line is too far away from. No marks are awarded.**

Question 3 mark scheme

(a) Bandwidth

(b) 1 mark for each of the following points:
   ▷ More bandwidth is assigned to downloading than uploading…
   ▷ …because there is more demand for downloads.

(c) 1 mark for each of the following points:
   ▷ Variable signal quality between phone lines.
   ▷ Distance between modem and telephone exchange as 3 miles is the approximate limit.

   (Do not accept bandwidth without some expansion, e.g. number of users sharing the connection.)

Question 4
Student A

(a)

CABLE broadband internet access	True	False
They do not use traditional telephone lines to provide broadband internet access	✓	
Cable companies provide considerably more Mbps than are available with ADSL	✓	
A cable modem or router is not necessary for broadband internet access over cable		✓
Cable networks are a combination of coaxial copper cable and fibre optic cable	✓	
Making and receiving telephone calls will be affected by having cable broadband internet access		✓
Copper wires connect a house to the nearest connection point	✓	

ℰ **All the rows are correct. 6 marks**

(b) If the computer is connected to a remote server, the maximum speed of data transfer is the part of the connection with the lowest bandwidth. When the last part of the connection is reached to go to your house, there are old-type telephone wires that were originally meant to carry voice signals. At that point, going into the last stage the data speed slows down a lot, creating a 'bottleneck'.

ℰ **This is a full explanation. 3 marks**

Question 4
Student B

(a)

CABLE broadband internet access	True	False
They do not use traditional telephone lines to provide broadband internet access	✓	
Cable companies provide considerably more Mbps than are available with ADSL	✓	
A cable modem or router is not necessary for broadband internet access over cable		✓
Cable networks are a combination of coaxial copper cable and fibre optic cable	✓	
Making and receiving telephone calls will be affected by having cable broadband internet access	✓	
Copper wires connect a house to the nearest connection point	✓	

(e) This student loses 1 mark. Making and receiving telephone calls is not affected by having cable, as cable does not use traditional telephone lines. Therefore, the telephone line is not affected. **5 marks**

(b) The speed of data slows down a lot in the last part of its journey to your house and that is where the bottleneck occurs because the data have to go along ordinary wires.

(e) This is a good response as far as it goes, but there is no mention that the maximum speed of data transfer is governed by the part of the connection with the lowest bandwidth. **2 marks**

Question 4 mark scheme

(a) 1 mark for each row completed correctly.

CABLE broadband internet access	True	False
They do not use traditional telephone lines to provide broadband internet access	✓	
Cable companies provide considerably more Mbps than are available with ADSL	✓	
A cable modem or router is not necessary for broadband internet access over cable		✓
Cable networks are a combination of coaxial copper cable and fibre optic cable	✓	
Making and receiving telephone calls will be affected by having cable broadband internet access		✓
Copper wires connect a house to the nearest connection point	✓	

(b) 1 mark for each of the following points:
  ➢ (If a computer is connected to a remote server) the maximum speed of data transfer is the part of the connection with the lowest bandwidth.
  ➢ The bottleneck is usually the last connection between your house and the local telephone exchange…
  ➢ …because that is where the connection makes use of ordinary/old telephone wires designed to carry voice signals only.

Hints and tips

Look at the number of marks available for the question and try to make that number of different points.

Question 5
Student A

(a)

	Peer-to-peer network	Client–server network
They have no central server	✓	
Centralised security controls access to shared resources on servers		✓
Shared resources are kept on the server		✓
Each workstation on the network shares its files equally with the other workstations	✓	
Access to shared resources on the server is controlled		✓
There is no authentication of users	✓	
The server contains a list of usernames and passwords		✓
They offer better security		✓

☺ All ticks are correctly placed. **8 marks**

(b) The server controls the security on a client–server network, unlike on a peer-to-peer network where there is no central control of security.

☺ The difference is well explained. **2 marks**

Question 5
Student B

(a)

	Peer-to-peer network	Client–server network
They have no central server	✓	
Centralised security controls access to shared resources on servers		✓
Shared resources are kept on the server		✓
Each workstation on the network shares its files equally with the other workstations	✓	
Access to shared resources on the server is controlled		✓
There is no authentication of users	✓	
The server contains a list of usernames and passwords		✓
They offer better security	✓	

☺ The last tick should be for client–server network. **7 marks**

(b) The security is on the main server on a client–server network.

☺ The student loses a mark for not mentioning peer-to-peer networks. **1 mark**

Question 5 mark scheme

(a) 1 mark for each row completed correctly.

	Peer-to-peer network	Client–server network
They have no central server	✓	
Centralised security controls access to shared resources on servers		✓
Shared resources are kept on the server		✓
Each workstation on the network shares its files equally with the other workstations	✓	
Access to shared resources on the server is controlled		✓
There is no authentication of users	✓	
The server contains a list of usernames and passwords		✓
They offer better security		✓

(b) 1 mark for each of the following points:
> Client–server: the server controls security of the network.
> Peer-to-peer: there is no central control over security.

Question 6
Student A

(a)

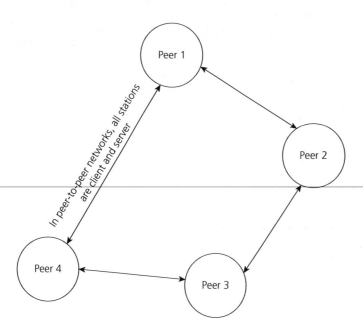

In peer-to-peer networks, all stations are client and server

ⓔ **All arrows are correct; the server is mentioned but the student has indicated that it applies to every station; individual stations are correctly labelled. 3 marks**

(b)

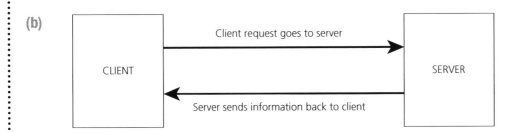

ℯ The arrows are the correct way (1); arrows are labelled correctly (1); an indication of client and server (1); and the diagram is correct overall (1). **4 marks**

Question 6
Student B

(a)

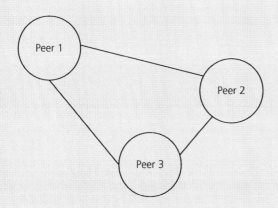

ℯ The stations are correctly labelled (1); no mark is awarded for arrows as only lines have been drawn and there is no overall mark for everything being correct. **1 mark**

(b)

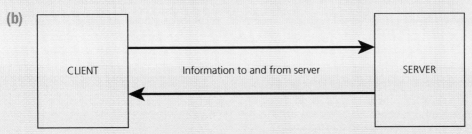

ℯ This student has correctly shown the client and server (the boxes can be the same size or different sizes) (1) and the arrow directions are correct (1). No marks are awarded for words near arrows because both arrows should be labelled and similarly there is no overall mark for the diagram as not everything is correct. **2 marks**

Question 6 mark scheme

(a) 1 mark for all arrows correct. 1 mark for sensible labelling of stations. 1 additional mark overall if everything else is correct.

Note:
⟩ It is not essential for the shapes to be circles.
⟩ The stations should be labelled in some way to indicate different peers, similar to those shown below.
⟩ The arrows should point both ways from one station to another, as shown below.
⟩ If the word 'server' is used in the diagram, it indicates that it applies to every station.

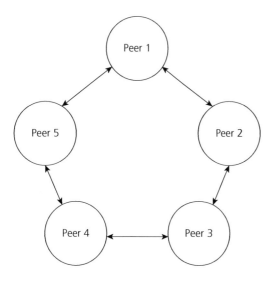

(b) 1 mark for each of the following points:
⟩ Correct client and server (the boxes can be shown the same size or different sizes).
⟩ Correct arrow directions.
⟩ Labels near/on arrows. The words do not need to be exactly the same as those given here, but they should be correct.
⟩ Overall if everything else is correct.

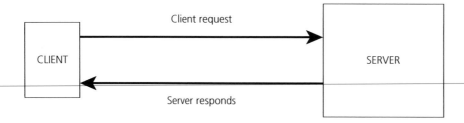

Question 7
Student A

(a) Hub or switch

ⓔ **This is correct on both counts, but only 1 mark is available. 1 mark**

(b) Router
Cabling
Modem

ⓔ **All correct. 3 marks**

(c) An analogue telephone line needs the modem to change the digital signal from the computer into an analogue signal so it can go down the phone line. At the other end, another modem changes it back again from analogue to digital so that the computer at the other end can understand it.

ⓔ **This is a concise explanation that meets all the criteria for full marks. 4 marks**

Question 7
Student B

(a) Bridge

ⓔ **This response is incorrect, so no mark is awarded.**

(b) Router
WiFi stuff
Network card

ⓔ **This loses a mark because 'stuff' is inappropriate. 2 marks**

(c) A modem can change the signal from digital to analogue and back again.

ⓔ **This is not an incorrect statement, but the question asks for an explanation and is worth 4 marks. 2 marks**

Question 7 mark scheme

(a) Hub or switch or hub/switch.

(b) 3 marks from:
▷ router
▷ cabling
▷ WiFi technology, e.g. access points
▷ network interface cards
▷ modem

(c) 1 mark for each of the following points:
▷ A computer's digital signal is changed into an analogue signal by the modem…
▷ … it/the analogue signal can then be sent/transmitted down the telephone line.
▷ When the signal is received, another modem changes the analogue signal back to digital…
▷ … to enable it to be understood by the receiving computer.

Question 8
Student A

(a)

	Switches	Routers
They can send and receive data at the same time	✓	
They can pass data between two networks		✓
They send data only to the computer for which they are intended	✓	
They provide built-in security such as a firewall		✓
They can be wireless		✓

ⓔ **All the rows are correct. 5 marks**

(b) (i) Wireless Access Point

(ii) It gives you access from a wired computer to a wired network.

ⓔ **Both the definition and the statement are correct. 2 marks**

Question 8
Student B

(a)

	Switches	Routers
They can send and receive data at the same time	✓	
They can pass data between two networks	✓	
They send data only to the computer for which they are intended	✓	
They provide built-in security such as a firewall		✓
They can be wireless	✓	✓

ⓔ **The second tick is placed incorrectly and the final row has a tick in both boxes. 3 marks**

(b) (i) Wired Access point

(ii) It lets you access other people's networks anywhere.

ⓔ **The definition is incorrect and the statement is too vague in part (ii), so no marks are awarded.**

Question 8 mark scheme

(a) 1 mark for each row completed correctly.

	Switches	Routers
They can send and receive data at the same time	✓	
They can pass data between two networks		✓
They send data only to the computer for which they are intended	✓	
They provide built-in security such as a firewall		✓
They can be wireless		✓

(b) 1 mark for each of the following points:
  (i) Wireless Access Point
  (ii) It provides wireless access to a wired ethernet network/it lets computers or devices connect to a network wirelessly.

Question 9
Student A

(a) Network Interface Card

ⓔ **This response is correct. 1 mark**

(b) An NIC is what connects a computer to a computer network.

ⓔ **This response is correct. 2 marks**

(c) Fibre optics, copper wire, WiFi.

ⓔ **All valid examples. 3 marks**

Question 9
Student B

(a) Network Interactive Component.

ⓔ **This definition is wrong, so no mark is awarded.**

(b) An NIC is a circuit board inside a computer.

ⓔ **This response loses a mark because it does not say what is being connected. 1 mark**

(c) Cables and WiFi.

ⓔ **'Cables' is too vague and there are only two responses when three are expected. 1 mark**

Question 9 mark scheme

(a) Network Interface Card or Network Interface Controller.

(b) Examples of possible answers:
  ▷ An NIC is a hardware component that connects a computer to a computer network.
  ▷ An NIC is a circuit board/card inside a computer to connect to a network.

For 2 marks, the response must specify that it connects one thing to another.

(c) 1 mark for each of the following points:
  ▷ optical cables/fibre glass cables
  ▷ copper wires
  ▷ wireless

Question 10
Student A

(a) A wireless router and a wireless Network Interface Card (NIC).

ⓔ **This is a full answer. NIC has been nicely defined as well for a high-level response. 2 marks**

(b) You don't have to be at a specific place in your home or office in order to work via WiFi. It is simple to connect other gadgets to the WiFi network. If cables had to be installed, it would create a mess, take longer and cost more to do, therefore it is easier to connect with WiFi.

With WiFi you can get interference that you wouldn't have with a wired network and if your house has thick walls the distance that the signal travels could be more limited than it should be. There are possibilities of connections dropping easily and of hackers.

ⓔ **This student has given a clear response, listing four advantages and four disadvantages. 8 marks**

Question 10
Student B

(a) Router and NIC.

ⓔ **This student does not specify 'wireless' or 'WiFi' for either answer, so no marks are awarded.**

(b) You can get WiFi in lots of places. You don't have to sit at the same desk all the time. Your other devices can use the same WiFi and it is quite easy to set them up. You have to have a strong signal with WiFi to get it to other parts of the house and it can be slow.

ⓔ **Two advantages and two disadvantages are given. 4 marks**

Question 10 mark scheme

(a) 1 mark each for two of the following points:
  ➢ a WiFi router
  ➢ (a computer with) a WiFi adaptor/wireless NIC
  ➢ a modem
  ➢ a Wireless Access Point

(b) 1 mark for each advantage and disadvantage (to max. 8):
Advantages:
  ➢ You don't have to be at a specific location.
  ➢ The number of connections is not limited by the number of physical connection points.
  ➢ It is easier than having to install cables through the building.
  ➢ Set-up costs can be inexpensive compared to other methods.

Disadvantages:
  ➢ Wireless networks can get interference.
  ➢ Devices with wireless capabilities and the extra equipment required can be expensive.
  ➢ Connections can be unstable.
  ➢ If the signal needs to go through walls, it can lose quality.

▷ There is the possibility of hacking.
▷ They are slower than networks that are wired.

Question 11
Student A

(a) Domain Name System

ⓔ **The definition is correct. 1 mark**

(b) Normally you have an address for where you want to go to on the internet, such as www.anyaddress.com, but a DNS server works with numbers. It keeps the URLs and their associated numbers in a huge database and they are called an IP address. It finds the IP address that matches your www address and routes you to the correct site.

ⓔ **This is concise but accurate. 4 marks**

Question 11
Student B

(a) Domain Name Server

ⓔ **The student should have said system, not server. No mark is awarded.**

(b) A DNS finds the number to match the website you want and uses it to send you there. It is called an IP address.

ⓔ **Two correct points are made. 2 marks**

Question 11 mark scheme

(a) The correct answer is Domain Name System.

(b) 1 mark for each of the following points (to max 4):
▷ It turns domain names (such as www.mydomainname.co.uk) into numbers…
▷ …(because numbers are more difficult to remember compared to URLs.)
▷ The IP address is used to route you to the requested site.
▷ The DNS looks at its own database to find the IP address…
▷ …if it cannot locate it, it queries another DNS so it can find the domain name you requested.

Hints and tips
There are 4 marks available, so try to mention four different points in your explanation.

Question 12
Student A

An Internet Protocol (IP) address is a number allocated to a device on a network. The IP addresses are allocated dynamically and can be reused.

ⓔ **This is a full and accurate response. 2 marks**

Question 12
Student B

An Internet Protocol (IP) address is a number linked to a device.

ⓔ **This student has correctly stated that an IP address is a number linked to a device but goes no further. 1 mark**

Question 12 mark scheme

2 marks from:

▷ An IP address is a unique identifier for a device on a network.
▷ It is represented by four numbers between 0–255/ 4 octets (separated by dots).
▷ If it is a v6 IP address it will be represented by hexadecimal digits (eight groups of four digits separated by colons).
▷ An IP address is assigned at a logical level (and so can be changed).
▷ IP addresses are unique so devices can be individually identified and communicated with on a network.

Hints and tips

There are 2 marks, so try to find two different points to make when you are writing your answer.

Question 13
Student A

(a) If I have written a web page, I need to have it hosted so that others can go there. For this I will need a web server. There are many hosting companies that let you upload your website to their servers. That would mean my website was being 'hosted'.

ⓔ **This is an accurate response and there are additional comments that clarify the response. 1 mark**

(b) You need a good speed for uploading your site whenever you make changes and people who view it need a good response time to download it quickly. You need help and tools if something goes wrong or you need help to buy more space.

ⓔ **The student loses a mark because there is no explanation for tools. 7 marks**

Question 13
Student B

(a) There are web hosting firms that sell you space on their servers.

(e) **A mark is given for mentioning web hosting firms. 1 mark**

(b) Help, speed, response time, tools.

(e) **Four factors are listed, but there is no description. 4 marks**

Question 13 mark scheme

(a) To make a website available for others to see (by placing it on the host's servers).

(b) 2 marks for each of the following points (to max. 8):
- Help: if things go wrong or you need to ask about something.
- Cost: how much is charged for the hosting package.
- Bandwidth: is there a limit to the amount of data that can be downloaded in the process of people accessing your site?
- Type of hosting: shared hosting, dedicated server or virtual private server.
- Tools: such as being able to see how many people visit your site.
- Speed: a good upload speed as you may need to update and upload many times.
- Response time: for visitors to your site who will not wait if downloading a page takes too long.

Question 14
Student A

(a) Data can be stored in the cloud as well as backups.

(e) **Two other valid uses of cloud computing are given. 2 marks**

(b) It is less expensive to use the cloud for accessing applications because the company or individual only pays for the software applications they need. It would also save the technician time to install the software and to keep it upgraded as that would be done automatically. Different employees can access the same document from anywhere as long as they have internet access.

(e) **This is a complete response. 4 marks**

Question 14
Student B

(a) Store data and backup.

(e) **This gives enough information to gain 1 mark, but the response could have been amplified for better understanding. 1 mark**

(b) You can back up to the cloud. You can use the software in the cloud from any computer with access to the internet. Software from the cloud gets upgraded automatically.

(e) **No mark is awarded for the first part of the response because no advantage is included. The second and third parts of the response are correct. 2 marks**

Question 14 mark scheme

(a) 2 marks from:
> To back up data
> To store data
> Carry out large amounts of processing
> To allow collaborative work

(b) 1 mark for each of the following points:
> It saves space: data can be automatically backed up to the cloud/you don't have to use space on the hard disk for applications software.
> Access: employees can work from anywhere with internet access.
> Maintenance costs: these are lower because there is no need to install and maintain software/upgrades are performed automatically.
> Collaboration: employees can use the same document as they are not kept on a computer.

Question 15
Student A

(a) Data ownership may be unclear if it is on a remote server, so it would be safer on a bank's own server as they could use a 'need-to-know' system of access to various data.

(e) **This is a well explained and correct response. 2 marks**

(b) Advantages:

> You don't need to buy software that you aren't using and you can use computers anywhere to work on, either in the organisation or anywhere in the world where you have an internet connection.
> The software is updated online.
> The backup situation is an advantage as you don't need to waste space on your own system and data backed up in the cloud with a reliable provider can have better reliability.
> Software in the cloud gives compatibility across browsers and different devices.

Disadvantages:
- You need a network connection.
- Having your data online might not be secure and there may be copyright issues around the original data.
- You may need to buy more storage as well.
- You may be disadvantaged if you need to do something that the online software does not have but that the full version does.

e **This is a clear discussion of advantages (cost, flexibility, reliability, backup) and disadvantages (security, storage, software). 7 marks**

Question 15
Student B

(a) Someone else may access the data if it is in the cloud and it would be safer on their own server.

e **This response is not specific enough. 1 mark**

(b) The advantages are that you don't need a lot of storage space on your own PC and it could work out cheaper for a business if they only buy the exact software they need. They would not need to use a technician's time either to install and update the software.

The disadvantages are that you may have your data stolen by hackers if you keep it online and you may have a problem with copyright.

e **3 marks are awarded for discussing the advantages (storage, software cost, maintenance costs) and 2 marks for the disadvantages (security, copyright). 5 marks**

Question 15 mark scheme

(a) 2 marks from:
- There may be ambiguity to the ownership of data stored in a publically owned cloud server.
- They could impose extra restrictions to data held if they are on their own cloud server.
- The organisation may have little control over the country in which data is stored (which may have legal ramifications).

(b) 10 marks from the following points (1 mark each):

Advantages:
- Software cost: you only have to buy what you need to use/some freely available via web apps.
- Maintenance cost: a technician is not needed to update and install software.
- Flexibility: you can use different computers anywhere to work on.
- Reliability: software and browsers are updated online/you don't have to download updates.
- Backup: if data are backed up in the cloud with a provider (who is reliable), this can be more reliable than storing them on a hard drive or USB flash memory.
- Compatible: there is compatibility across browsers and different devices.

Disadvantages:
- Connections: you can only access information if a network connection is available.
- Secure: data stored online can be vulnerable to security attacks.

> Storage: storage online can be limited (unless more is bought)/it is possible to buy much more physical storage to save information on at home.
> Copyright: there is a chance of losing rights to original work if it is stored online.
> Software: not all software through online apps has the same functions/facilities.

Hints and tips

This question is worth 10 marks, so try to find five advantages and five disadvantages.

Question 16
Student A

(a) You can install a virtual services switch and link into it, via the internet, all the computers, devices and peripherals, such as printers, that may be in different geographical locations. It then appears as if they are in your office rather than at another location.

ⓔ **This is a clear statement of how you can connect to a virtual network and an example of how it appears. 3 marks**

(b)

	True	False
A VLAN is configured through software	✓	
A virtual network link is neither a wired nor a wireless connection	✓	
You cannot store or retrieve data over a virtual network		✓
Virtual networking is a standard feature of some versions of MS Windows	✓	

ⓔ **Each row is correct. 4 marks**

Question 16
Student B

(a) A virtual network links computers that are in other places via the internet by using a hardware switch.

ⓔ **A brief statement that is an adequate description of virtual networking, but the student does not mention how it appears. 2 marks**

(b)

	True	False
A VLAN is configured through software	✓	
A virtual network link is neither a wired nor a wireless connection	✓	
You cannot store or retrieve data over a virtual network		✓
Virtual networking is a standard feature of some versions of MS Windows		✓

ⓔ **The last row is incorrect. 3 marks**

Question 16 mark scheme

(a) 1 mark for each of the following points:
- ⋙ Virtual networking is a technology allowing the control, over the internet, of remotely located computers...
- ⋙ ...it consolidates them on to a single hardware component which is called a virtual services switch.
- ⋙ It enables data to be stored and retrieved, software to be run and peripherals to be operated through a web browser just as if the remote computers are onsite.

(b) 1 mark for each row completed correctly.

	True	False
A VLAN is configured through software	✓	
A virtual network link is neither a wired nor a wireless connection	✓	
You cannot store or retrieve data over a virtual network		✓
Virtual networking is a standard feature of some versions of MS Windows	✓	

Question 17
Student A

Costs are reduced because maintenance can be carried out on remote machines from a central location and users can access data, software and resources from any part of the system as if they were on the same LAN.

ⓔ **This is a valid response. 2 marks**

Question 17
Student B

Costs and less hardware to buy.

ⓔ **'Costs' is not explained separately, but the rest of the response, taken with the word 'costs', is worthy of a mark. 1 mark**

Question 17 mark scheme

2 marks from:
- ⋙ The central control reduces costs...
- ⋙ ...since maintenance can be carried out on remote machines from a central location...
- ⋙ ...and users can access resources from various remote sites.
- ⋙ There may be less hardware and software required since access to this can be shared over the virtual network.

1.5 Network topologies, protocols and layers

Question 1
Student A

(a) (i) Star (ii) Mesh

ⓔ **Both answers are correct. 2 marks**

(b) In a star network, it is easy to connect new nodes and to detect and troubleshoot a failure but if the central hub fails, then all of the nodes fail. The performance is dependent on the capacity of the central hub.

In a mesh network, other nodes can handle traffic if one node fails. It can cope with a high amount of traffic. They are high cost compared to other topologies and difficult to maintain.

ⓔ **The student identifies the two networks individually, listing two advantages and two disadvantages for a star network as well as two advantages and two disadvantages for a mesh network. 8 marks**

Question 1
Student B

(a) (i) Star (ii) Network

ⓔ **'Star' is correct, but 'Network' is incorrect (it should have been 'Mesh'). 1 mark**

(b) Advantages
- Easy to connect new computers.
- Easy to detect a failure.
- All the computers depend on the central hub working properly.

Disadvantages
- Data transmitted from all devices at the same time.
- Makes lots of traffic possible.

ⓔ **Listing responses is a good way to approach this question. 5 marks**

Question 1 mark scheme

(a) 1 point for each correct answer:
- (i) is a star.
- (ii) is a mesh.

(b) 1 mark for each of the following points (8 marks max.):
Advantages of a star topology
- With star topology it is a simple task to connect new nodes or devices; new nodes can easily be added and not affect the rest of the network; components can also be removed easily.
- The centralised management makes monitoring the network straightforward.
- The failure of one of the nodes does not affect the rest of network.
- It is easy to detect a failure.

 OCR GCSE (9–1) Computer Science Exam Question Practice

Disadvantages of a star topology
- Because the network depends on the central hub…
- … if the central hub fails, then the entire network fails.
- The cost of the network is increased if a hub/router/switch is used as a central device.
- The capacity of the central hub dictates the performance and number of nodes that can be dependent on it.

Advantages of a mesh topology
- If one node fails then the network traffic can be redirected to other nodes therefore the whole network will not fail.
- Data can be transmitted from different devices simultaneously.
- A mesh topology can support high traffic.
- If a component fails, an alternative can be used so that data transfer is not affected.
- Nodes are unaffected by expansion and modification being carried out.

Disadvantages of a mesh topology
- High chances of redundancy in many of the network connections.
- In comparison to other topologies, the overall cost is high.
- Set-up/maintenance/administration can be difficult.

Hints and tips

List responses and make sure that you are clear which topology you are referring to.

Question 2
Student A

(a) Each separate computer is connected to a central hub. The hub controls the whole network and acts as a junction to connect different nodes.

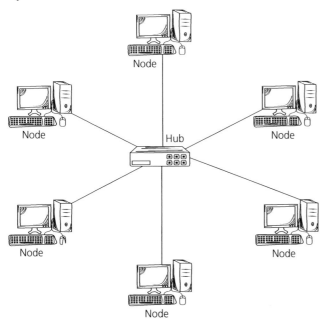

This response merits 2 marks for the diagram with labels correct and 3 marks for the description. The labels could be node/client/computer and hub/server. **5 marks**

(b) Each separate computer is connected to every other device on the network by a point-to-point connection to all devices. Each node can send out its own signals and relay signals of other nodes on the network.

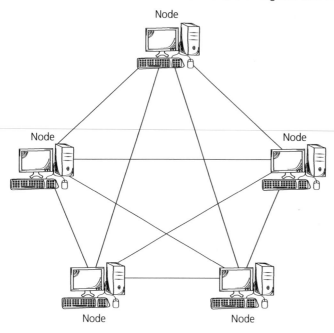

(e) This response merits 2 marks for the diagram with labels correct and 3 marks for the description. The labels could be node/client/computer. **5 marks**

Question 2
Student B

(a) There is one server in the middle and lots of computers around and every computer is connected to the one in the middle.

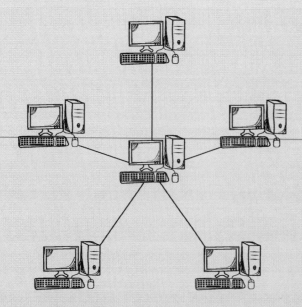

(e) This response merits 1 mark for the diagram without labels and 2 marks for the description. **3 marks**

(b) All the computers are connected to all of the others.

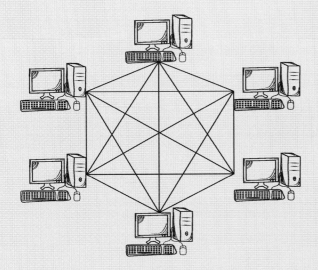

(e) This response merits 1 mark for the diagram without labels and 1 mark for the description. **2 marks**

Question 2 mark scheme

(a) 1 mark for an appropriate diagram and 1 mark for the correct labelling of the diagram. 3 marks for any of the items in the following list or another appropriate response:

▷ Each node/client/computer is connected to a central hub/server.
▷ It uses a point-to-point connection (to central device).
▷ The central hub can be a computer server/hub/router/switch.
▷ Hub acts as junction to connect the different nodes.
▷ Hub manages and controls whole network.

(b) 1 mark for an appropriate diagram and 1 mark for the correct labelling of the diagram. 3 marks for any of the items in the following list or another appropriate response:

▷ Each node/client/computer is connected to all of the other devices/all devices are interconnected...
▷ ...by a point-to-point connection to every other node.
▷ Each node/client/computer can send its own signals and relay data from other nodes.

Question 3
Student A

(a) Wireless networks use **radio** waves.

In a WiFi network, the device that sends and receives radio signals is the **router**.

A **wireless** router should be centrally placed in your home for the best possible range.

Most laptops have a **Wireless Network Interface Card** built in.

ⓔ **This student has entered the correct terms. 4 marks**

(b)

Statements	True	False
A WiFi network is faster than a cabled network		✓
The speed of a WiFi network is influenced by the strength of the radio signal	✓	
A wireless router cannot make a connection with a physical network		✓
A WiFi connection is more stable than a wired network		✓
A wireless adaptor converts data into a radio signal	✓	
A wireless receiver also converts data into a radio signal		✓
It costs a lot less to add extra hardware to a WiFi network		✓

ⓔ **All rows are correct. 7 marks**

(c) The advantages are that a wireless network means you don't have to be at home or school to get a connection and you don't have to have any wires or cables hanging around or any extra hardware and it is inexpensive to start.

On the other hand, you can get interference on a WiFi system and sometimes if you go out of range, or if you have thick walls in your house, the connection stops.

ⓔ **Seven good points made across advantages and disadvantages. 7 marks**

Question 3
Student B

(a) Wireless networks use **radio** waves.

In a WiFi network, the device that sends and receives radio signals is the **router**.

A **wireless** router should be centrally placed in your home for the best possible range.

Most laptops have a **wireless** built in.

ⓔ **Only the first, second and third sentences are correct. 3 marks**

(b)

Statements	True	False
A WiFi network is faster than a cabled network	✓	
The speed of a WiFi network is influenced by the strength of the radio signal		✓
A wireless router cannot make a connection with a physical network	✓	✓
A WiFi connection is more stable than a wired network		✓
A wireless adaptor converts data into a radio signal	✓	
A wireless receiver also converts data into a radio signal		✓
It costs a lot less to add extra hardware to a WiFi network		✓

e **The first two rows are incorrect and the third row is ticked for both options. 4 marks**

(c) It doesn't cost much, there are no wires and you can be anywhere. Sometimes you can't get a signal if you are not at home.

e **There is 1 mark for 'no wires', but no mark for 'It doesn't cost much' as the cost needs to refer to the setup being inexpensive. The comment 'you can be anywhere' is not enough to gain the mark. A mark is awarded for 'if you are not at home'. 2 marks**

Question 3 mark scheme

(a) 1 mark for each term correctly entered:

Wireless networks use **radio** waves.

In a WiFi network, the device that sends and receives radio signals is the **router**.

A **wireless** router should be centrally placed in your home for the best possible range.

Most laptops have a **Wireless Network Interface Card** built in.

(b) 1 mark for each row completed correctly.

Statements	True	False
A WiFi network is faster than a cabled network		✓
The speed of a WiFi network is influenced by the strength of the radio signal	✓	
A wireless router cannot make a connection with a physical network		✓
A WiFi connection is more stable than a wired network		✓
A wireless adaptor converts data into a radio signal	✓	
A wireless receiver also converts data into a radio signal		✓
It costs a lot less to add extra hardware to a WiFi network		✓

(c) 1 mark for each of the following points (to max. 8):

Advantages
- Initially inexpensive to set up.
- No requirement for a specific location.
- No extra hardware is needed in order to connect up multiple devices.
- No extra wires are needed.

Disadvantages
▷ Interference can easily occur in a wireless network.
▷ Connection is less stable than it is for a wired network.
▷ Can lose quality through walls or obstructions.
▷ More possibility of hacking.
▷ A wireless network connection can be slower than for wired networks.

Question 4
Student A

(a) Ethernet means a network communication standard that can handle large amounts of data at high speeds.

ⓔ **This is a full and accurate response. 2 marks**

(b) It states how many conductors are required for a connection and the performance to be expected.

ⓔ **Both points made are correct. 2 marks**

(c) It can transmit data at 100–1000 Mbps (megabits per second).
It is easy to install.
It is comparatively low cost.
It supports popular network protocols.
It is reliable because it checks if anyone else is transmitting and, if so, waits a short time to prevent a possible collision.
It is evolving all the time to higher transmission speeds.
It is reliable because it uses either twisted pair or fibre optic cabling.
It is not affected by the environment around it and not is subject to signals being disrupted.

ⓔ **All the points made in this response are correct. 8 marks**

Question 4
Student B

(a) Ethernet is a protocol that handles large amounts of data.

ⓔ **This response gains 1 mark for 'handles large amounts of data'. The first part of the response is too vague to gain a mark. 1 mark**

(b) WAN and LAN.

ⓔ **This student seems to have made an incorrect guess at a correct response, so no marks are awarded.**

(c) It is low cost and has a simple design.

ⓔ **Ideally, the first part of the response should say 'comparatively low cost' or include a comparison, but there is enough here for 1 mark. A second mark is not awarded as having a simple design needs an expansion. 1 mark**

Question 4 mark scheme

(a) 2 marks from:
- Network communication standard.
- It can handle large amounts of data.
- Network hardware and the way data is handled are defined by the standard.
- It uses an open protocol at the application layer.
- It is the network cards and cabling needed for high speeds.

(b) 1 mark for each of the following points:
- It defines network hardware.
- It defines the network protocol/how data is to be handled.

(c) 1 mark each for the following point (to max. 8):
- It can transmit data at 100–1000 Mbps (megabits per second).
- It is easy to install.
- It is comparatively low cost…
- …because of its simple design.
- It can support popular network protocols.
- It checks if anyone else is transmitting and, if so, it waits a short time to prevent a possible collision; this reduces errors and failed transmissions.
- It is evolving all the time to higher transmission speeds/functional requirements.
- It uses twisted pair or fibre optic cabling which provide a reliable fixed connection.
- It has high immunity from electrical noise from outside sources.

Question 5
Student A

(a)

Acronym	Definition	Description
TCP/IP	Transmission Control Protocol/Internet Protocol	Used to transfer data over a network
FTP	File Transfer Protocol	Transfers files from one host to another
POP	Post Office Protocol	Used by email clients to retrieve email from remote server over a TCP/IP connection
IMAP	Internet Message Access Protocol	It leaves your email messages in your ISP mail server so you can read the emails on any computer
SMTP	Simple Mail Transfer Protocol	It moves email across networks, sending it to the right computer and mail box

ℯ This defines all the acronyms correctly (5) and supplies appropriate descriptions (5). **10 marks**

(b) MAC addresses are permanently on the hardware and IP addresses can be changed depending on the TCP/IP network.

ℯ This is an accurate response. **2 marks**

(b) http:// HyperText Transport Protocol is for information to be passed between web servers and clients.

https:// HyperText Transfer Protocol Secure can be used to upload credit card payments in online shopping.

ℯ This is a complete and accurate response. **4 marks**

Question 5
Student B

(a)

Acronym	Definition	Description
TCP/IP	Transmission Control Protocol	Breaks data down into small packets
FTP	File Transfer Protocol	Transfers files from one host to another
POP	Post Office Protocol	Used in email
IMAP	Internet Message And Protocol	It leaves your email messages in your ISP mail server so you can read the emails on any computer
SMTP	Secure Mail Transfer Protocol	It moves email across networks

ⓔ **This provides correct definitions for FTP and POP (2) and correct descriptions for FTP, IMAP and SMTP (3). 5 marks**

(b) MAC address can't be changed, IP can.

ⓔ **This student correctly states that a MAC address cannot be changed, but no mark is awarded for 'IP can' as it is not a complete statement. 1 mark**

(c) They are both the same, but https means it's secure.

ⓔ **This is a fairly well written response, but it makes only one point. 1 mark**

Question 5 mark scheme

(a) 1 mark for each correct definition and 1 mark for each correct description.

Acronym	Definition	Description
TCP/IP	Transmission Control Protocol/Internet Protocol	A collection of protocols used for transferring data over a network/the internet.
FTP	File Transfer Protocol	Allows files to be uploaded and downloaded from a server.
POP	Post Office Protocol	Used by email clients to retrieve email from a server and then deletes them from the server.
IMAP	Internet Message Access Protocol	Allows users to download emails and arrange the folders in which they are stored. (Ensures the email client reflects the server and as such does not delete emails in the download process.)
SMTP	Simple Mail Transfer Protocol	Used for *sending* emails. (Clients often use POP3/IMAP to receive emails and SMTP to send them.)

Hints and tips
Check your definitions carefully. For the descriptions, try to keep your responses short and to the point.

(b) 1 mark for each of the following points:
  ➤ The MAC address is fixed to the device hardware and cannot be changed (physical).
  ➤ The IP address for the same device can be changed (logical).

(c) 1 mark for each of the following points:
  ➤ http stands for HyperText Transport Protocol.
  ➤ It is a protocol for information to be passed between web servers and clients. (i.e. the transmission of webpages).
  ➤ In https, the s stands for 'secure' (HyperText Transfer Protocol Secure).
  ➤ It indicates no one can eavesdrop as the website sends data in an encrypted form.

Question 6
Student A

(a) How communication is established and terminated
Methods of data compression
How data errors will be detected and corrected

ⓔ **This student missed a possible mark for the format of data to be exchanged. 5 marks**

(b) TCP breaks up the data and puts it into packets to be transmitted together with their destination address and IP routes the packets individually to their destination and puts them back into the right order once they arrive.

ⓔ **This is a clear description worthy of full marks. 2 marks**

(c) Every message gets broken down into something called data packets, which go by the best available route at any particular millisecond and therefore they may not all travel together. It doesn't matter what route the packets take as TCP/IP makes sure that the packets arrive at the correct address and will reassemble them into their correct order. This is possible because each packet contains the packet identification details, source address, destination address and the data.

ⓔ **Six separate, valid points have been made. 6 marks**

Question 6
Student B

(a) How computers communicate with each other
How to compress data
How to find errors

ⓔ **The first response is too vague, so no mark is awarded. The other two points are both valid responses. 3 marks**

(b) They send packets of data over the internet.

ⓔ **This is not specific enough, so no marks are awarded.**

(c) A message is turned into data packets that are sent across the internet network, but not all at the same time. When they arrive, they are put together again, into one message.

ⓔ **This student states that a message is broken down into data packets (1) and sent across the network, but not all at the same time (1). The second sentence is enough to gain a mark. 3 marks**

Question 6 mark scheme

(a) 1 mark for each of the following points:
- ⊳ How communication will be established between machines
- ⊳ How communication will be terminated between machines
- ⊳ How to check for errors
- ⊳ How any errors will be corrected
- ⊳ Transmission speed
- ⊳ How data is compressed for speedier transmission

(b) 1 mark for each of the following points:
- ⊳ TCP creates and maintains a connection across which data can be transmitted.
- ⊳ IP splits data into packets that can then be transmitted (and reassembled at their destination).

(c) 1 mark for each of the following points:
- ⊳ A message is broken down into data packets…
- ⊳ …and each packet travels by the best available route at any particular millisecond…
- ⊳ …so they may not all travel together.
- ⊳ The route does not matter as TCP/IP ensures that the packets arrive at the correct address…
- ⊳ …and will assemble them into their correct order.
- ⊳ This is possible because each packet contains the packet identification details, source address, destination address and the data.

Question 7
Student A

(a) Application, transport, network, link.

ⓔ **This is a correct response. 4 marks**

(b)

Description	Layer name
The MAC address information to specify sending and receiving hardware devices	Link
It encodes the data being transmitted	Application
Adds the IP addresses of the sender and recipient	Network
The data is divided into manageable chunks	Transport

ⓔ **Each row is correct. 4 marks**

(c)   Each separate layer carries out a specific function.

One layer can be changed without affecting the other layers.

Simplifies the model as it is divided into parts according to their function.

Easier to find and correct network errors/problems.

Gives a standard for hardware and software manufacturers to follow.

e   **This is a perfect response. 5 marks**

Question 7
Student B

(a)   Transport layer
Internet layer

e   **Both responses are correct, but four responses are expected. 2 marks**

(b)

Description	Layer name
The MAC address information to specify sending and receiving hardware devices	Link
It encodes the data being transmitted	Application
Adds the IP addresses of the sender and recipient	Link
The data is divided into manageable chunks	Application

e   **Only two responses count, as there is duplication for other two. 2 marks**

(c)   Each layer has a different task to perform and that makes it simpler as any layer can be changed without affecting the other layers. This is a standard for everywhere so communication is achieved.

e   **This response makes three good points, but the student has not mentioned that the model is divided into parts and that it is easier to find and correct network errors/problems. 3 marks**

Question 7 mark scheme

(a)   1 mark for each of the following points:
   ⤳ Application layer
   ⤳ Transport layer
   ⤳ Network layer/internet layer
   ⤳ Link layer/network access layer

(b)   1 mark for each row completed correctly.

Description	Layer name
The MAC address information to specify sending and receiving hardware devices	Link/network access
It encodes the data being transmitted	Application
Adds the IP addresses of the sender and recipient	Network/internet
The data is divided into manageable chunks	Transport

(c) 1 mark for each of the following points:
   ▷ Each separate layer carries out a specific function.
   ▷ One layer can be changed without affecting the other layers.
   ▷ Simplifies the model as it is divided into parts according to their function.
   ▷ Easier to find and correct network errors/problems.
   ▷ Gives a standard for hardware and software manufacturers to follow to achieve communication.

Question 8
Student A

(a) Packet number
Total length
Destination address
Sender address
Checksum
Protocol

ⓔ **This is a correct response, but only five fields are asked for. 5 marks**

(b) The data packets are sent separately and travel by different routes from router to router along the way depending on which routes are the best and not too busy. Each packet has a destination address and when they all arrive they are put back together in accordance with the packet sequence number contained in the header.

ⓔ **Six valid points are made. 6 marks**

(c) It uses the network efficiently so there are no holdups.
It is secure as it is very difficult to intercept a whole message.

ⓔ **Only two advantages are given. 2 marks**

Question 8
Student B

(a) Where it is going to
Where it came from
Number

ⓔ **The first two responses are adequate for addresses (2), but the third is not specific enough to know what the number corresponds to. 2 marks**

(b) They are marked with a number and a destination address so when they arrive they can be put together in the right order. If one packet doesn't arrive, an error message is sent to the computer it came from as the packet also has the address it came from on it.

ⓔ **This response is explained well but could be expanded. 4 marks**

(c) It makes the best use of the network to get there quickly.

ⓔ **This is good enough for 1 mark, but other advantages are missed. 1 mark**

Question 8 mark scheme

(a) 5 marks from:
- Protocol
- Source address
- Destination address
- Packet number
- Checksum
- Total length
- Time to live if not delivered

(b) 1 mark for each of the following points:
- Packets leave source computer to go through network.
- Each packet has its destination address.
- As packets are sent off separately, they will travel towards their destination on different routes…
- …depending on which route is least busy at any particular millisecond.
- Re-directed by routers to the next router with the fastest connection.
- When packets arrive, they are put together in the right order…
- …according to their packet sequence number.
- If a packet does not arrive, a message is sent to the source computer to ask for a replacement.

(c) 1 mark for each of the following points:
- It makes efficient use of the network/does not tie up the network.
- It is more secure/more difficult to intercept messages.
- It is fault tolerant (if part of the network goes down packets can be sent via alternate routes.)

1.6 System security

Question 1
Student A

Finding gaps in the computer system or network where an attacker could get in and then attempting to patch the system and make sure it is configured correctly to keep it secure. When new technologies or applications are created it is best to pen test them before they go into production. Staff training for security team. To test new hardware and software and to discover new bugs in existing software.

🄮 **This student has given a full and accurate response. 6 marks**

Question 1
Student B

Making sure the computer system cannot be hacked by trying to hack it yourself. Could be used to train new staff. To make sure that the computer system is set up correctly. Find weaknesses.

🄮 **This student has given a naturally expressed response, particularly for the first sentence. The following statement is too vague for a mark and would have been improved by defining 'new staff' as 'new security staff'. The third sentence is valid. The last point is too vague. 2 marks**

Question 1 mark scheme

1 mark for each of the following points (to max. 7):

▷ Find holes/vulnerabilities/backdoors before an attacker does.

▷ Verify that the computer system is configured securely.

▷ Find gaps in compliance/perform an audit of security.

▷ Test any new technologies or applications before they go into use.

▷ Can be used to train security staff/network technicians (not just 'staff').

▷ To discover new bugs in existing software.

▷ To find weaknesses in hardware and application software and people, then develop controls.

▷ To comply with any legal (or regulatory requirements).

Question 2

Student A

(a) To monitor and analyse data packets to try to detect any intrusions to the network.

ⓔ **This is a valid response. 2 marks**

(b) They can actually record data so that it can be analysed so that a voice over internet message could be analysed live.

It can find the source of data leaks and monitor the users to check that they are working within the IT policy rules.

ⓔ **This is a well-communicated, accurate response. If the student had remarked on the ability to troubleshoot intermittent network problems, they might have had an opportunity to gain the final mark. 3 marks**

(c)

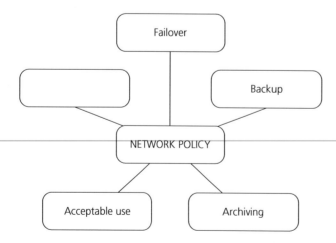

ⓔ **This student adds four appropriate issues. 4 marks**

Question 2
Student B

(a) It analyses computer network traffic.

(e) **If this student had stated for what purpose, they might have had an opportunity to gain the second mark. 1 mark**

(b) It monitors the employees using the network to make sure they are not breaking any company rules. It can identify where any data leaks are coming from.

(e) **This student has given two valid responses. 2 marks**

(c)

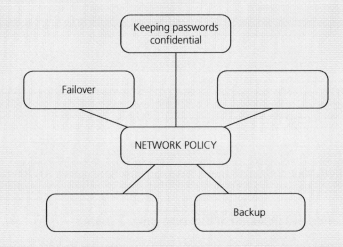

(e) **'Keeping passwords confidential' could be part of acceptable use. 3 marks**

Question 2 mark scheme

(a) 1 mark for each of the following points:
  - ▷ It relates to the monitoring/analysis of computer network traffic…
  - ▷ …to find evidence of a security attack.

(b) 1 mark for each of the following points:
  - ▷ To troubleshoot intermittent problems that occur on a network (at certain times).
  - ▷ To monitor activity of users to ensure they are complying with the organisation's policies.
  - ▷ To identify source of data leaks.
  - ▷ To enable replaying and analysing of VoIP/video over IP transmissions/live call data.

(c)   1 mark for each label in the following figure (in no particular order).

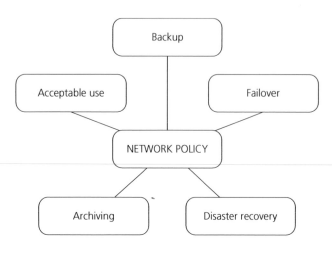

Question 3
Student A

(a)   It finds any malware and gets rid of it from your computer, then repairs any damage caused by the malware.

🄮   **The three steps in dealing with malware are included in this response. 3 marks**

(b)   A firewall can be hardware or software that filters incoming network traffic in order to provide security. You program it to what you will allow in and out. When you install a firewall you can set up what you want to allow in or out through the firewall. This prevents attackers from entering your system to carry out malicious damage.

🄮   **This student has evidenced a good knowledge of how a firewall works. Five of the seven criteria have been met. 5 marks**

(c)   A firewall can be a hardware device or software but anti-malware is only software. They both provide security, in different ways. The firewall filters incoming and outgoing network traffic, and you can set up what goes in or out of the network when the firewall is installed. The anti-malware prevents software being installed without you knowing. It can detect malware on a computer, but a firewall wouldn't let it in in the first place. A firewall prevents attackers from maliciously accessing your server whereas anti-malware may detect and remove it, once it is there.

🄮   **This student has given some good comparisons, making nine points. 9 marks**

Question 3
Student B

(a)   It gets rid of malware and viruses.

🄮   **This student has made just one point. 1 mark**

(b) It stops malware coming into your computer system. It intercepts communications between your computer and the outside in order to help block malicious connections. A firewall is placed between your computer and any network that you are connected to.

ⓔ **Three good basic points have been made, but the student is missing the fact that a firewall can be a hardware device or a software program. If they had known this, their response might have appeared more confidently written. 3 marks**

(c) A firewall goes between your computer and the network but the anti-malware software is installed on your computer.

Firewall gets rid of unwanted network communication and anti-malware gets rid of Trojan horses.

A firewall is software program that provides network security.

ⓔ **The last response has no comparison, so gains only 1 mark. If they had said that a firewall is a software program or a hardware device, it would have gained another mark. 5 marks**

Question 3 mark scheme

(a) 1 mark for each of the following points:
  ➢ Can detect malware on a computer.
  ➢ Safely removes malware.
  ➢ Cleans up any damage the malware caused to the computer.

(b) 1 mark for each of the following points:
  ➢ Can be a hardware device or a software program…
  ➢ …that provides network security.
  ➢ It is placed between your computer and any network you are connected to.
  ➢ Filters incoming and outgoing network traffic…
  ➢ …based on a set of rules defined by the user.
  ➢ Reduces or eliminates unwanted network communication and allows required information to flow freely.
  ➢ Prevents attackers from maliciously accessing your server.

(c) There should be comparisons between the two, with points made such as the following. 1 mark for each point (to max. 10).

Firewall:
  ➢ Can be a hardware device or a software program…
  ➢ …that provides network security.
  ➢ It is placed between your computer and any network you are connected to.
  ➢ Filters incoming and outgoing network traffic…
  ➢ …based on a set of rules defined by the user.
  ➢ Reduces or eliminates unwanted network communication and allows required information to flow freely.
  ➢ Prevents attackers from maliciously accessing your server.

Anti-malware software:

▷ Stops software installing without your knowledge.

▷ Can detect malware on a computer.

▷ Safely removes malware.

▷ Cleans up any damage the malware caused to the computer.

▷ Protects against many types of infections caused by viruses, worms, Trojan horses, rootkits, spyware, keyloggers.

▷ Can be installed on an individual computer/gateway server/dedicated network appliance.

Question 4
Student A

(a) Keep the network secure by allowing only some employees to access different levels of information. This also helps to ensure that there is no un-licensed software put onto the network.

🄴 This is a good response that goes further than just 'stating' what is meant; it explains as well. **2 marks**

(b)

Type of permission	Network manager	User
Install software	✓	
Remove software	✓	
Can only access particular software in work area		✓
Access all user areas	✓	
Change permissions	✓	
Can manage account users	✓	

🄴 All ticks indicate the correct response. **6 marks**

(c) How many different levels are needed.

Who can only view items.

Who can edit or delete items.

What software programs a user needs to use.

🄴 This response meets all the criteria for full marks. It would have been better to have worded the response in the context of the question, i.e. 'Michael will have to decide the following questions:'. **4 marks**

Question 4
Student B

(a) Depending on their job in an organisation, different workers have only got access to some things on the network.

🄴 This is a good answer, but the student did not mention software licensing. **1 mark**

(b)

Type of permission	Network manager	User
Install software	✓	
Remove software	✓	
Can only access particular software in work area	✓	
Access all user areas	✓	
Change permissions	✓	
Can manage account users	✓	

e The third row is incorrect. **5 marks**

(c) Michael will have to decide who can do what and what they have access to on the network.

e The response has been nicely put into context but only 'what they have access to on the network' gains a mark. The rest is too vague to gain further marks. **1 mark**

Question 4 mark scheme

(a) 1 mark for each of the following points:
- It is a hierarchical method where access to data/programs/activity at different levels in the hierarchy are defined to help to keep the network secure…
- …and that unlicensed software cannot be installed on the network.

(b) 1 mark for each row completed correctly.

Type of permission	Network manager	User
Install software	✓	
Remove software	✓	
Can only access particular software in work area		✓
Access all user areas	✓	
Change permissions	✓	
Can manage account users	✓	

(c) 1 mark for each of the following points:
- What a user can view/edit/delete.
- What software a user will need to have access to.
- What files on the network the user will need to have access to.
- How many different access levels are required.

Question 5
Student A

To be able to access documents stored securely in her user area and to use the software she needs to work on them.

The use of passwords helps to keep the whole network secure.

ⓔ **This response evidences the student's knowledge, including that the use of passwords only 'helps' to keep the network secure. The student loses a mark by not mentioning being able to access the company's documents stored on the network. 4 marks**

Question 5
Student B

So she can work on her documents stored in her user area and get the right software to use.

ⓔ **This is a basic response, but both points are correct. 2 marks**

Question 5 mark scheme

1 mark for each of the following points:
- To keep her documents secure.
- To access the documents stored in her user area.
- To make sure she can access company documents stored on the network.
- To be able to use the software she needs for her work.
- To keep the network secure.

Question 6
Student A

(a) Encryption uses a key to encrypt data into ciphertext and the person you send it to needs the same key to decrypt it.

ⓔ **This is a sound response. 2 marks**

(b) Decryption means using a key to turn the ciphertext back into plaintext so it can be read and understood.

ⓔ **This is a correct and clear response. 1 mark**

(c) The computer sending the document encrypts it. This method uses two keys at once, a private key and a public key. The sending computer is the only one that knows the private key but the public key is given by the sending computer to any other computer that wants to communicate with it securely.

The public key and its own private key are used to decode the message by the receiving computer. Although the public key used for encryption is available to anyone, they still can't read it without the private key.

Prime numbers are used for the key pair because there are a great many prime numbers and therefore a great many different key codes can be used.

ⓔ **This is a high-level response listing nine of the ten possible points. 9 marks**

Question 6
Student B

(a) Encryption means changing the data into something that cannot be read using a code.

ⓔ **This response has missed mentioning ciphertext and the wording of the response is slightly unclear, but enough has been said to gain a mark. 1 mark**

(b) You have got to have the code.

ⓔ **The response indicates that the student knows what decryption means, but they have not managed to explain the question, so no mark is awarded.**

(c) You send encrypted messages with a private key and when the computer that you have sent the message to gets the private key, it can decrypt and read the message. There is a public key and a private key that are used. The encryption is based on prime numbers.

ⓔ **This student has accurately stated the four points in their response; they know that prime numbers are used but have not expanded into why. 4 marks**

Question 6 mark scheme

(a) 1 mark for each of the following points:
  ▷ Encryption describes the process of translating data from plaintext into 'data' that looks like it is nonsensical and random…
  ▷ …which is called ciphertext.

(b) Decryption describes the process of converting ciphertext back to plaintext.

(c) 1 mark for each of the following points:
  ▷ The document is encrypted by the sending computer.
  ▷ Two different keys used/combination of private key and public key used.
  ▷ The private key is only known by your computer…
  ▷ …the public key is given by your computer when any computer wants to establish a secure communication.
  ▷ For the message to be decrypted/decoded, a computer must use the public key that was provided by the originating computer and its own private key/a computer must use both keys.

▷ As the public key used for encryption is available to anyone, the message sent from one computer to another will not be secure…

▷ …but anyone who sees it can't read it because they haven't got the private key.

▷ The receiving computer uses the same key to encode/decode/read the document.

▷ The key pair is based on prime numbers of long length.

▷ As there are a huge number of prime numbers, the possibilities for different keys are vast.

Question 7
Student A

(a) Trojans

Rootkits

Worms

Spyware

ⓔ **This is a clear response. 4 marks**

(b) Phishing is trying to lure you into giving away private information such as bank details by sending an email that looks as if it came from your bank. Or they could take over your identity to commit other fraudulent actions.

ⓔ **This is a good answer listing three of the four possible responses. 3 marks**

(c) This isn't a computer-based method of fraud because it is based on the non-technical method of approaching a person and treating them as the weak link in the system. Fraudsters often use psychological or emotional methods to trick that person into giving away secure information that they would not normally divulge.

ⓔ **This student makes four excellent points. 4 marks**

Question 7
Student B

(a) Trojans

~~Worms~~

Viruses

ⓔ **Viruses is a repeat as there is already a shape containing this name. 2 marks**

(b) Criminals try to get your personal details so they can steal from you or get your personal identity to commit fraud.

ⓔ **The response is in the general area but has made only two points. 2 marks**

(c) It gets a person to give away security information that they would not normally do by getting them to think there is an emergency or by scaring them.

ⓔ **This student makes two points. 2 marks**

Question 7 mark scheme

(a) 1 mark for each of the following labels:
  - Trojans
  - rootkits
  - worms
  - spyware

Or another appropriate answer.

(b) 3 marks from:
  - An email is sent from a seemingly legitimate source (e.g. a bank).
  - The email will contain a request to follow a link…
  - …usually there is a sense of urgency to encourage the user to click the link (e.g. a warning of suspicious activity on the account).
  - The link will take the user to a website that will look like an official site (but is actually owned by the scammer).
  - When the user attempts to log into the fake site it stores their login details.

(c) 4 marks from:
  - It attempts to scare a person into giving information or by clicking on a link.
  - It tries to get the victim to give away sensitive information that they would not otherwise give…
  - …by attempting to invoke fear/urgency by using psychological/emotional manipulation.
  - It is a non-technical method of gaining fraudulent information by tricking people into breaking normal security procedures.
  - It treats a person as the weak link in an otherwise secure system.

Question 8
Student A

(a) A brute-force attack is run automatically by a computer program to try to get into your encrypted password list, or other file, by trying out endless password possibilities.

e **The response is given correctly and is well deserving of full marks. 2 marks**

(b) You only get three chances to enter your correct password, so trying millions of passwords wouldn't work. Some places ask you to type in the number you see in an image to make sure that you are a real person and not a computer program. Some sites ban the IP addresses of those attempting to log in too often.

e **All responses are valid. 3 marks**

(c) Lots of failed logins from the same IP address or trying lots of different usernames from one IP address. Sometimes there is an attempt to login to the same account from lots of different IP addresses or when passwords are tried in dictionary/alphabetical order.

e **This is a good response to a difficult question, but the student loses 1 mark by not mentioning excessive bandwidth consumption. 4 marks**

Question 8
Student B

(a) It tests out a list of passwords to try to get into your files.

℮ **A basic response that nevertheless gains a mark. 1 mark**

(b) After the third try you cannot try any more passwords.

℮ **Only one way to prevent a brute-force attack is given. 1 mark**

(c) When you try to log in three times, it blocks you out. Many different usernames have been tried against the same password.

℮ **The first point is too vague, so no mark is awarded. The student needs to amplify this point to include 'from the same IP address'. The second point is valid. 1 mark**

Question 8 mark scheme

(a) 1 mark for each of the following points:
   ▷ It runs a series of every possible password to attempt to unlock your file…
   ▷ …which is done by using a computer program that runs automatically.

(b) 3 marks from:
   ▷ If you keep trying different passwords, you get blocked after three attempts.
   ▷ You get an image that you have to type in to verify that you are not a computer.
   ▷ IP addresses can be banned after multiple failed logins.
   ▷ You are asked for your response to a secret question.
   ▷ Enforce passwords of such length and complexity that all combinations can't feasibly be tried.
   ▷ Increase the time taken for the system to check a password.

(c) 1 mark for each of the following points:
   ▷ When the same IP address shows that it has made multiple failed logins.
   ▷ When many different usernames attempted to login from the same IP address.
   ▷ Login attempts for one account are from various IP addresses.
   ▷ High bandwidth consumption from a single use.
   ▷ When there are failed login attempts from usernames/passwords used alphabetically.

Question 9
Student A

(a) Denial of service.

℮ **This is the correct answer. 1 mark**

(b) When you type in a URL, if someone floods the network you are requesting to see your request will be denied because there is a limited number of requests that can be actioned at any one time. A similar attack can also happen on your email account because you only get a certain amount of data allowed in your email account at the same time and if the attacker sends you lots of email, you won't have any space left for legitimate email to be delivered.

ⓔ **This student states that flooding the network (1) can cause requests for service to be denied (1) because only a limited number of requests can be actioned at any one time (1). They then describe what can happen if an email account is attacked (3). 6 marks**

(c) Get anti-attack software for this sort of attack and buy a wide amount of bandwidth.

ⓔ **This response is not very well written, but nevertheless it meets the criteria for both marks. 2 marks**

Question 9
Student B

(a) DoS

ⓔ **This student names the attack correctly, albeit in abbreviated form. 1 mark**

(b) You can't get your emails because a lot of spam email has been sent to you and there is no room left for your own emails to be delivered.

ⓔ **This student makes two points relating to email attacks. 2 marks**

(c) If you have enough band width then you should be OK.

ⓔ **This is enough for 1 mark. Ignore the fact that bandwidth is written as 2 words. 1 mark**

Question 9 mark scheme

(a) Denial of service attack (DoS).

(b) 1 mark for each of the following points:
- The computer and network connection are targeted…
- …or the computer(s) and network of the site you want to access are targeted.
- The network is flooded with information so it cannot process your request…
- …because it can only process a fixed number of requests at one time.
- An attack can be spam emails to attack your email account…
- …because your email account has a quota allocated for the amount of data in your account at any time.
- An attacker can use up all of your quota so you cannot receive messages.

Hints and tips

Try to think through what happens in such an attack and write it out step by step.

(c) 1 mark for each of the following points:
- Purchase a lot of bandwidth.
- Use specific DoS attack detection technology.

Question 10
Student A

(a) Data sniffing.

e This is correct. No embellishment to the response is required to gain the mark. **1 mark**

(b) (i) Structured Query Language

(ii) When you are on a web page that has a database for you to use, you enter what you are searching for. This takes the format of an SQL statement that is written in text. Because it is text, a malicious hacker could inject their own SQL statement, which might be just a very small piece of code, into the search criteria and the hacker could get access to user names and passwords in a database.

e The definition is correct and this student gives a correct definition and a considered explanation for part (ii). **6 marks**

Question 10
Student B

(a) PA

e This is incorrect, so no mark is awarded.

(b) (i) ?

(ii) A hacker injects malicious code into a search of a database on a website.

e No mark is awarded for part (i). For part (ii), this student makes two valid points. **2 marks**

Question 10 mark scheme

(a) The correct answer is one of: (data) sniffing/eavesdropping/packet sniffing/packet analyser.

(b) (i) Structured Query Language

(ii) 1 mark for each of the following points:
- ▷ A website takes user input (for example from textboxes).
- ▷ When this is submitted it is sent to the server and used in an SQL statement to query a database.
- ▷ Commands can be entered in a specific way into the user input form.
- ▷ When they are used in the SQL statement they are carried out along with the original statement.
- ▷ This can be used to retrieve, add or delete data into the database in an unauthorised way.

Question 11
Student A

(a) (i)   Confidentiality relates to access to information being for authorised persons only.

    (ii)   This means that any information needs to stay in its intended form.

    (iii)   Availability means that information should always be available to any authorised person.

ℰ **This student gives an accurate response to each part of the question. 3 marks**

(b)

FORMS OF ATTACK ON NETWORKS		
	PHISHING	It is a crime to try to find sensitive information, such as passwords or bank details, by fraud.
	SNIFFER ATTACK	Data interception and the theft of packets, as if they are written in plain text they can be read and interpreted.
	PASSWORD-BASED ATTACK	They keep trying to duplicate a valid logon or password.
	DENIAL OF SERVICE ATTACK	An attacker attempts to prevent legitimate users from accessing information or services/an attacker floods the requested URL with many requests so yours cannot be dealt with.
	BRUTE-FORCE ATTACK	You can get software to try out all possible passwords until the correct one is found.
	SQL INJECTION	Injection of a small piece of code to change a database search made online by a user.
	POOR NETWORK POLICY	Networks need a network policy to set out rules for integrity, confidentiality and accessibility to keep the network safer.
	MALWARE	Software that has been designed to sniff out personal information on a computer.
	PEOPLE AS THE WEAK POINT IN A SECURE SYSTEM	Scaring people to give up confidential information.

ℰ **All the descriptions are correct. 9 marks**

Question 11
Student B

(a) (i)   Confidentiality means keeping the information secure.

    (ii)

    (iii)   Availability means that it can't be available to everyone.

ℰ **The first part is not enough to gain a mark because it needs to say that any information is for authorised people only. The last part is just about enough to gain a mark. 1 mark**

(b)

	PHISHING	A criminal who tries to find passwords and bank details, by fraud.
	SNIFFER ATTACK	Data packet interception.
	PASSWORD-BASED ATTACK	Try lots of different passwords to get in.
	DENIAL OF SERVICE ATTACK	This is about not giving the URL.
FORMS OF ATTACK ON NETWORKS	BRUTE-FORCE ATTACK	You can get software to try out all possible passwords until the correct one is found so you can corrupt a system.
	SQL INJECTION	
	POOR NETWORK POLICY	Networks in large places have to have a network policy.
	MALWARE	Software that has been designed to find out personal information on a computer.
	PEOPLE AS THE WEAK POINT IN A SECURE SYSTEM	Scaring people to give up their information.

ⓔ **The first three descriptions are enough for a mark each. The 'denial of service attack' response is not full enough to gain a mark, although the student is along the right lines. 'SQL injection' has not been answered. The information about network policies is not enough to gain a mark. 6 marks**

Question 11 mark scheme

(a) 1 mark for each of the following points:

▷ Confidentiality: only people who are authorised have access to this specific information.

▷ Integrity: information should remain in the form in which it was originally intended.

▷ Availability: those authorised should always have access to the information.

(b) 1 mark for each correct description added to the boxes.

	PHISHING	A criminal activity that tries to find sensitive information, such as passwords or bank details, by fraudulent methods.
	SNIFFER ATTACK	Data interception and theft/data packets written in plain text can be read, intercepted or hijacked.
	PASSWORD-BASED ATTACK	Repeated attempts made to duplicate a valid logon or password.
	DENIAL OF SERVICE ATTACK	An attacker attempts to prevent legitimate users from accessing information or services/an attacker floods the requested URL with many requests so yours cannot be dealt with.
FORMS OF ATTACK ON NETWORKS	BRUTE-FORCE ATTACK	Software that tries out all possible passwords until the correct one is found.
	SQL INJECTION	Injection of a small piece of code to change a database search made online by a user.
	POOR NETWORK POLICY	(Corporate) networks need a sound network policy to set out rules for integrity, confidentiality and accessibility (without which a network may be vulnerable).
	MALWARE	Software that has been designed to sniff out personal information on a computer (such as spyware, root-kits, adware).
	PEOPLE AS THE WEAK POINT IN A SECURE SYSTEM	Manipulating/scaring people to give up confidential information.

Question 12
Student A

(a) Permission

 This is a correct response. 1 mark

(b) 1 Reconnaissance.
2 Identification of where it is vulnerable.
3 Try to break in.
4 Report on what you found.

 This is an excellent response. There is nothing wrong with listing points. 4 marks

Question 12
Student B

(a) The tester is not a hacker.

ⓔ **This student seems to be thinking along the right lines, but the response is inadequate, so no mark is awarded.**

(b) Try to break into the system.
Tell management if you managed it or not.

ⓔ **Two valid points are made. 2 marks**

Question 12 mark scheme

(a) A tester has permission and a hacker does not.

(b) 4 marks from:
- ⊳ Research the target and…
- ⊳ …look for potential vulnerabilities.
- ⊳ Set up an attack and…
- ⊳ …carry out the attack.
- ⊳ Test the ability to recover any compromised data after the attack.

1.7 Systems software

Question 1
Student A

(a) You can enter commands into a GUI by pointing and clicking on icons on the screen. This sends the operating system off to open the item you clicked on which could have been a file or an application. A command line interface just has a screen prompt and you have to type in commands that you have to know.

ⓔ **A fourth mark could have been gained had the student said more about CLI. 3 marks**

(b)

Comparisons	CLI	GUI
User-friendliness	Need to remember many different commands	Much more visually intuitive New users find it easier and faster to use/learn than a CLI
Diversity	Commands remain the same	Different GUIs have different design changes between versions
Multi-tasking	Some CLIs can multi-task, but are not as able to see multiple things at once on one screen	GUI can use windows to view lots of programs or folders at same time
Speed of operating	Only need to use keyboards so quicker to operate than GUI	Use of a mouse and a keyboard makes it slower for someone who is familiar with and working in a command line
System resources	Uses less of a computer's system resources than a GUI	Needs more system resources

(e) The last row for the GUI column needs expansion as to why more system resources are needed. **9 marks**

Question 1
Student B

(a) GUI is WIMP and a command line is just a flashing cursor.

(e) **The response is almost there for a CLI mark but not quite enough to evidence adequate knowledge. No mark is awarded.**

(b)

Comparisons	CLI	GUI
User-friendliness	Difficult to learn and remember lots of commands	Easier and faster to learn than a CLI
Diversity		What you have to click on might change as new versions come out
Multi-tasking	CLIs can't multi-task as well as a GUI	You can open lots of different windows at once
Speed of operating	Only need to use keyboards	Using a mouse as well as a keyboard can slow people down
System resources		

(e) **The CLI response for multi-tasking is weak as it doesn't say why you can't multi-task as well as on a GUI, so no mark is awarded. Also, no marks are awarded for missing answers. 6 marks**

Question 1 mark scheme

(a) 1 mark for each of the following points:
  ▷ A graphical user interface (GUI) allows commands to be entered by pointing at and click on icons or objects that appear on-screen…
  ▷ …for the user to interact with the operating system of an application.
  ▷ A command line interface (CLI) displays a screen prompt where the user types in commands…
  ▷ …for each task they want to perform and receives a response back.

(b) Mark in pairs of comparisons (CLI and GUI) for 2 marks each.

Comparisons	CLI	GUI
User-friendliness	Not very user-friendly as you need to remember lots of different commands/need to be familiar with how it works and how to navigate. New users will probably find it more difficult than a GUI.	Much more visually intuitive/you can often guess what to click on. New users find it easier and faster to use/learn than a CLI.
Diversity	Commands remain the same (even if new ones are added to them).	Different GUIs have different designs for different/multiple changes between versions. You need to find out where everything is in a new, changed version.
Multi-tasking	Some CLIs can multi-task, but not as well as a GUI, as the ability to see multiple things at once on one screen is not as good.	GUIs use windows to view/manipulate multiple programs/folders at the same time.
Speed of operating	You only need to use the keyboard.	Requires the use of a mouse and is much slower for someone who is familiar with working in a command line.
System resources	Uses less of a computer's system resources than a GUI.	A GUI needs more system resources as e.g. icons/fonts/drivers need to be loaded so that takes more system resources than CLI.

Hints and tips

Write something into each box that compares the same thing for a CLI and a GUI. Try to give reasons for what you say.

Question 2
Student A

(a) Bootstrapper
Utility software
Device drivers
BIOS
GUI
Linkers

ⓔ Saying 'bootstrapper' instead of 'bootloader' is acceptable. **6 marks**

(b)

Term	Definition
Command line interface	A way of interacting with a computer via a keyboard input at a screen prompt.
Device driver	A driver is a program that controls devices such as printers.
Utilities	System software that can analyse, configure, optimise and maintain a computer.
Linker	It takes files generated by a compiler and then combines them into a single file that can be executed.
Graphical user interface	An interface between the user and the computer, communicating by clicking on icons using a mouse or trackpad.
Compiler	It converts source code into a language that can be understood by a computer.

ⓔ All definitions are correct. **6 marks**

Question 2
Student B

(a) BIOS
Utility software
Disk defragmenter
A user interface

ⓔ 'Disk defragmenter' is too specific; it needed to be 'Utility software'. **3 marks**

(b)

Term	Definition
Command line interface	You type in a command at a screen prompt
Device driver	A program that works devices
Utilities	Things like disk defragmenter and optimisation
Linker	It links the user to the computer
Graphical user interface	WIMP
Compiler	It compiles programs

ⓔ The definitions for Linker and GUI are too weak for a mark, and the response for Compiler is too vague. **3 marks**

Question 2 mark scheme

(a) 6 marks from:
> Loads programs
> Linkers
> Device drivers
> Utility software
> User interface
> BIOS/basic input and output system
> A hypervisor
> A bootloader

(b) 1 mark for each row completed correctly.

Term	Definition
Command line interface	An interface displaying a prompt where a command can be entered by the user. When the command is input, it is displayed next to the prompt and then executed when <Enter> is pressed.
Device driver	A software program that is needed by external hardware devices to make them function with the operating system of the computer, e.g. a printer.
Utilities	Software programs that can add functionality to your computer; they analyse the performance of a computer and help it to perform better; they help to keep date secure and perform file management tasks.
Linker	A program that can combine object files generated by a compiler into one file.
Graphical user interface	Software that enables a user to interact with the computer by pointing and clicking graphic elements such as icons, scroll bars, menus etc. in order to input commands.
Compiler	A software program that takes the source code of a program and translates it into machine language or code so that it can be executed.

Question 3
Student A

(a) Controls **peripherals** such as scanners and printers.
Responsible for the transfer of programs in and out of **memory**.
Organises the use of memory between **programs**.
Organises **processing time** between programs and users.
Maintains **security** and access rights of users.
Deals with **errors** and user instructions.
Allows the user to save files to a **backing store**.
Provides the **interface** between the user and the computer.

ⓔ **All entries are correct. 8 marks**

(b) The file you want to save, or write, to hard disk is now larger. Looking at the above diagram, the grey cells are allocated. This means that they are already being used by another file. But the spaces left unallocated, or not used, are not big enough to store the file.

The file would be saved in the first 4 white cells, then the rest of the file would be stored in the next free cell or cells shown in white and so on. Like this the one file may be split up and stored across many different locations in storage. This is called a discontiguous file because it is in pieces.

ⓔ **All points made are correct. 4 marks**

Question 3
Student B

(a) Controls _____ such as scanners and printers.

Responsible for the transfer of programs in and out of **backing store**.

Organises the use of memory between **programs**.

Organises **processing time** between programs and users.

Maintains _____ and access rights of users.

Deals with **errors** and user instructions.

Allows the user to save files to a **backing store**.

Provides the **memory** between the user and the computer.

ⓔ **The first and fifth sentences are missing a response and the second sentence should have 'memory' instead of 'backing store'. The last sentence should be 'interface' not 'memory'.**
4 marks

(b) Now the file is bigger, if there isn't enough free space all together in one place to store it, it gets split up and stored in different memory locations.

ⓔ **This student has made two valid points. 2 marks**

Question 3 mark scheme

(a) 1 mark for each term entered correctly.

Controls **peripherals** such as scanners and printers.
Responsible for the transfer of programs in and out of **memory**.
Organises the use of memory between **programs**.
Organises **processing time** between programs and users.
Maintains **security** and access rights of users.
Deals with **errors** and user instructions.
Allows the user to save files to a **backing store**.
Provides the **interface** between the user and the computer.

(b) 1 mark for each of the following points:

⊳ If there is not enough contiguous space to store a file, the file may become separated and stored across more than one location/The storage medium does not have enough unallocated space in one place to store the file/The spaces left unallocated/unused are not big enough to store the file.

⊳ The rest of the file would be stored in the next free cell or cells.

⊳ If that space is not large enough to store the whole file, it may be split up and stored across many different locations in storage.

⊳ This is called a discontiguous file.

Question 4
Student A

(a) Multi-tasking is when you are running several programs at the same time on your computer like spreadsheets and word processing.

As the processor can only fetch and execute one instruction at a time, the operating system keeps all the programs open, even though only one can be executed at a time. The other programs wait for their turn to be executed by the processer, which can swap the turns super-quick. To the user it always seems that all of the applications are open, so that is why it is called Multi-tasking.

ⓔ **This is a full response, but this student loses a mark because they do not say that the operating system allocates which programs have their turn to be executed and when. 7 marks**

(b) To make sure that RAM is used efficiently, it transfers items in RAM to secondary storage when not currently needed and retrieves them from secondary storage to RAM when they are needed again.

Manages virtual memory.

ⓔ **This student has made four valid points. 4 marks**

Question 4
Student B

(a) Multi-tasking is when you can listen to music while doing your word processing homework.
Because the CPU can only fetch and execute one instruction at a time, the OS keeps both of the programs open and switches quickly between the two and others if they are open.

ⓔ **Six valid points. 6 marks**

(b) When programs or files are needed to go into RAM it allocates free space to them. Manages virtual memory.

ⓔ **Two valid points. 2 marks**

Question 4 mark scheme

(a) Look for the following points in the response (1 mark each, up to 8 max.):
- The computer can run several programs at the same time…
- …for example, listening to music while using another application or browsing the internet.
- The processor can only fetch and execute one instruction at a time…
- …so for multi-tasking, the operating system keeps all the programs open even though only one is being executed currently.
- All other applications/programs are waiting for their turn to be executed.
- The processor then gives each program a turn to be executed…
- Multiple cores working on different programs.
- …it swaps the turns very quickly between programs…
- …so to the user it looks as if all programs are running at the same time.
- The operating system allocates which programs have their turn to be executed and when.

Hints and tips

Think about how multi-tasking works, what the processor can or cannot do and what the operating system has to do to help and to make it appear to the computer user that they are running lots of programs at once. Try to work through the process step by step, making different points.

(b) 4 marks from:
- Ensures RAM used efficiently.
- Manages virtual memory.
- Transfers items in RAM to secondary storage when not currently needed.
- Retrieves items in secondary storage to RAM when needed.
- Monitors which areas in RAM are used and what is stored there.
- Allocates free space in RAM to a program or file.

Or any other appropriate task.

Question 5
Student A

(a) Create folders.
Delete or rename files.
Move files from one folder to another.
Copy/paste files to another disk (for backup).
Transfer files across the internet using ftp.

🅮 **This is a full and accurate response. 5 marks**

(b) The file allocation table is updated to show where the file can be located.

🅮 **This is a correct and succinct response. 1 mark**

Question 5
Student B

(a) Make folders.
Delete files.
Move files to different folders.

e **The student could name only three of the five tasks. 3 marks**

(b) The file is moved to the new folder.

e **This response is incorrect. The file is not physically moved; only the FAT is updated. No mark is awarded.**

Question 5 mark scheme

(a) 5 marks from:
  ▷ Create folders.
  ▷ Organise by date, type or filename etc.
  ▷ Show as large or small icons, lists or extended lists.
  ▷ Delete or rename files.
  ▷ Move files from one folder to another.
  ▷ Copy/paste files to another disk (for backup).
  ▷ Transfer files across the internet using FTP.

(b) The entry in the FAT/file allocation table/index is updated to show the new location of the file.

Question 6
Student A

(a)

✓	FAT is updated
✓	User moves or copies and pastes the file to a new folder
	File is physically moved from one folder to the other

e **The correct items have been selected. 2 marks**

(b) ▷ Each user logged into the system and their workspace
  ▷ Allocates resources to jobs a user wants to run
  ▷ For each user, keeps logs of how much processing time and resources they use
  ▷ Works out most efficient use of computer processing cycles
  ▷ Maintains security

e **This student provides a full response. A response does not have to be in essay format for computer science; in this case, bulleted points are a more appropriate way of presenting the response. 5 marks**

Question 6
Student B

(a)

	FAT is updated
✓	User moves or copies and pastes the file to a new folder
	File is physically moved from one folder to the other

ⓔ **The file is not physically moved, so no mark is awarded for this response. 1 mark**

(b) It manages the log in and keeps each user's work secure.

ⓔ **This student has made two valid points. 2 marks**

Question 6 mark scheme

(a) 1 mark for each row completed correctly

✓	FAT is updated
✓	User moves or copies and pastes the file to a new folder
	File is physically moved from one folder to the other

(b) 1 mark for each of the following points:
- Manages users logged in and their workspace.
- Allocates resources to jobs to be run.
- Keeps logs of processing time and resources used.
- Makes most efficient use of computer processing cycles.
- Maintains security.

Question 7
Student A

(a)

	Utility software?
Anti-virus software	✓
Applications software such as spreadsheets	
Bootloader	
Security programs	✓
Network programs	✓
Disk repair	✓
BIOS	
Backup facilities	✓

ⓔ **This student gives the correct responses. 5 marks**

(b)

Utility	Description
File viewer	To display the contents of a file
Disk defragmenter	Reorganises files and unused space on a disk
Compression	To shrink the size of a file
Backup utility	Copies files or an entire disk onto another disk or tape
Diagnostic utility	Compiles technical information about a computer and reports on any identified problems
Screen saver	Shows a moving image on screen when no keyboard activity has occurred for a specific time

ℯ Each description is worthy of a mark. **6 marks**

Question 7
Student B

(a)

	Utility software?
Anti-virus software	
Applications software such as spreadsheets	✓
Bootloader	✓
Security programs	✓
Network programs	
Disk repair	✓
BIOS	✓
Backup facilities	

ℯ This student gives two correct responses: security programs and disk repair. **2 marks**

(b)

Utility	Description
File viewer	To display the contents of a file
Diagnostic utility	Reorganises files and unused space on a disk
Compression	To shrink the size of a file
Backup utility	Copies files or an entire disk onto another disk or tape
Disk defragmenter	Compiles technical information about a computer and reports on any identified problems
Screen saver	Shows a moving image on screen when no keyboard activity has occurred for a specific time

ℯ Disk defragmenter and diagnostic utility are the wrong way round. **4 marks**

Question 7 mark scheme

(a) 1 mark for each correctly inserted tick.

	Utility software?
Anti-virus software	✓
Applications software such as spreadsheets	
Bootloader	
Security programs	✓
Network programs	✓
Disk repair	✓
BIOS	
Backup facilities	✓

(b) 1 mark for each row completed correctly.

Utility	Description
File viewer	To display the contents of a file
Disk defragmenter	Reorganises files and unused space on a disk
Compression	To shrink the size of a file
Backup utility	Copies files or an entire disk onto another disk or tape
Diagnostic utility	Compiles technical information about a computer and reports on any identified problems
Screen saver	Shows a moving image on screen when no keyboard activity has occurred for a specific time

Hints and tips

Fill in the ones you know first. Then carefully consider what is left and which are the best matches. Take your time.

Question 8
Student A

Your data become scrambled by using a large digital number called a key. This makes it possible to send a message without anyone else being able to read them unless they have the key.

⊘ This response is correct. **4 marks**

Question 8
Student B

The original data are scrambled with a digital key so that no one else can read them without the secret key.

⊘ This response is enough to gain 3 marks, but it is an area that the student could focus on for revision. **3 marks**

Question 8 mark scheme

(a) 4 marks from:
- The data will be scrambled/it scrambles the original message…
- …with a large digital number/key.
- Makes it possible to send a message without anyone else being able to read it…
- …unless they have the key.
- The computer receiving the message knows the digital key and so is able to work out the original message.
- The digital key is known by the receiving computer so it can read the original message.

Question 9
Student A

(a) When files are saved they are sometimes put in different places on a disk. If you run the defragmenter, it puts all the pieces back into one place so it is quicker for you when you want to load up the file.

e **This is a good explanation. 2 marks**

(b) Contiguous files means all of the file is in one place on the disk so there is faster data access.

e **This is a clear and accurate response. 2 marks**

Question 9
Student B

(a) When you run the defragmenter, it sorts out all the pieces and stores them in one place.

e **No marks are awarded because this student did not specify 'all the pieces' of what.**

(b) The bits of a file get split up so it gets slow to load up a file.

e **This student gains a mark for 'slow to load up a file', but the rest is too vague. 1 mark**

Question 9 mark scheme

(a) Accept a description such as the following (1 mark each):
- Disk defragmentation is when somebody puts all of the parts of a file into one place/contiguously on a storage device…
- …this process makes it quicker to load up a file/therefore the storage device can work more efficiently.

(b) Award marks either for the first 2 marking points or for the second 2 marking points.
- If a lot of files become discontiguous the computer slows down because…
- …it has to look in many different places on the storage device to find all the parts in order to open the file.

or

- A contiguous file will be held all in one place on the storage device…
- …so the file can be opened more quickly (than if it was held discontiguously).

Question 10
Student A

(a) Figure 7 is lossless and Figure 8 is lossy compression.

(e) **Both parts of the response are correct. 1 mark**

(b) Lossless compression reduces file size with no loss of information and when it arrives at the other end it is uncompressed to be the same as the original file. Algorithms are used to create reference points for recurring patterns and the algorithms are sent with the compressed file so they can be used to reconstruct the file.

Lossy compression permanently deletes unnecessary data so when it is decompressed it is not the same as its original file.

(e) **This student makes a good attempt at a thorough response. To get full marks, they should have added that a lossy compression file would still be viable. 7 marks**

Question 10
Student B

(a) They are both lossless.

(e) **This response cannot gain a mark as the student needs to link the responses to the figures.**

(b) Lossy:
  > Reduces files with no loss of information during the process…
  > …enables the original file to be recreated exactly when uncompressed.
  > Algorithms are used to create reference points for recurring textual patterns…
  > …these are stored and sent with the (now smaller) encoded file.
  > When the file is uncompressed it is reconstructed by using the reference points to put back the original information.

Lossless:
  > Eliminates some bits of information to reduce the file size/it permanently deletes unnecessary data.
  > Data will still be viable
  > The original file is not retained.

(e) **This is a full response, but lossy and lossless are the wrong way round. No marks are awarded.**

Question 10 mark scheme

(a) The correct answer is:
  > Figure 7 is lossless.
  > Figure 8 is lossy.

Both must be correct for the mark.

(b) 1 mark for each of the following points (to max. 4):

Lossless

▷ Reduces file size with no loss of information during the process…

▷ …enables the original file to be recreated exactly when uncompressed.

▷ Algorithms are used to create reference points for recurring textual patterns…

▷ …these are stored and then sent with the (now smaller) encoded file.

▷ When the file is uncompressed it is reconstructed by using the reference points to put back the original information.

Lossy

▷ Eliminates some bits of information to reduce the file size/it permanently deletes unnecessary data.

▷ Data which is considered redundant (e.g. frequencies that cannot be heard, differences in colour that cannot be discerned) is removed.

▷ The when uncompressed the new file will look/sound very close to the original but will not be bitwise identical.

Question 11
Student A

(a) Full backup and incremental backup.

ⓔ **This is a correct response. 2 marks**

(b) USB memory stick
Cloud-based services
Tape
Writable DVD/CD

ⓔ **This student has given four correct answers. 4 marks**

Question 11
Student B

(a) Backup on to a pen drive and on to an external hard disk.

ⓔ **The student has given possible backup media rather than stating 'types' of backup. No marks are awarded.**

(b) Memory stick
Tape
DVD
Hard drive

ⓔ **'Hard drive' is not specific enough – either external hard drive or hard drive on a different server would have attracted a mark. 3 marks**

Question 11 mark scheme

(a) 1 mark for each of the following points:
- full (backup)
- incremental (backup)

(Accept differential (backup)).

(b) 4 marks from:
- (USB) memory stick
- cloud-based services
- tape
- writable DVD/CD
- external hard drive
- different server

Question 12
Student A

(a) An incremental backup makes a copy of new or changed files since the last full backup, which makes it quicker than the full backup.

(b) A full backup makes a copy of everything on the system even if nothing has changed.

ⓔ **Each point made is correct. 4 marks**

Question 12
Student B

(a) An incremental backup just does anything that has changed.

(b) A full backup copies everything.

ⓔ **The first part of the response is too vague. It needs to specify 'changed' since when. 1 mark**

Question 12 mark scheme

1 mark for each of the following points:

Incremental backup
- Makes a copy of new or changed files since last full backup.
- Quicker than full backup.

Full backup
- Makes a copy of everything on the system…
- …even if unchanged since previous backup.

1.8 Ethical, legal, cultural and environmental concerns

Question 1
Student A

(a) Denise will need to consider the cultural issues relating to every country where the book is going to be distributed, such as not using images in the book that might be acceptable in the UK, but not in other countries.

The amount of political freedom in different countries varies a lot, so Denise will have to be careful not to include anything in her book that may be offensive to the Government of countries where political freedom is stricter than in others.

Colours used in the book will have to be considered carefully as some colours are difficult to see if the reader is colour blind.

ⓔ **This student has given valid three issues, with examples, but there is nothing on privacy.**

6 marks

(b) Hacking and hackers generally have a very bad reputation because they try to find a way into systems, sometimes called backdoors, so that they can steal or delete private data etc. But hackers can also be employed by large organisations to use their skills to test out systems so that they can close the backdoors and report to the organisations. They are sometimes used to find a way to work around programming bugs if it would be less costly than re-writing the original program. Good hackers, generally, might just warn the public that they could get hacked as their system is insecure.

ⓔ **The student has evidenced a rounded knowledge of this question. The final mark could have been gained if the student had mentioned looking for new ways to use a program or computer. 7 marks**

(c)

	✓ if an ethical issue
Your boss can read your work-related and your private emails sent during work time	✓
You have written a new app and given a copy to your friend who is using it without paying for it	
A teacher of a new subject has a responsibility to make sure they can do the job by getting trained in that subject	✓
A car crashes because of a problem with an embedded computer in a production run	✓

ⓔ **The ethical issues are identified correctly. 3 marks**

Question 1
Student B

(a) She needs to keep everything private while she is writing the book.
Cultural
Accessibility
Political freedom

(e) **The first sentence is too vague; 'everything' needs to be more specific. 'Cultural' is accepted, and the remaining issues are valid. However, this student has not provided any description. 3 marks**

(b) Hackers act against the law by breaking in to computer systems to steal personal data or to damage computer networks just because they want to. If a hacker was good they may tell people that they could be in danger.

(e) **It would be recommended that this student revise this subject area. The student knows the threat of hacking into a system, but is weak on how hackers may be employed for positive reasons. 3 marks**

(c)

	✓ if an ethical issue
Your boss can read your work-related and your private emails sent during work time	
You have written a new app and given a copy to your friend who is using it without paying for it	✓
A teacher of a new subject has a responsibility to make sure they can do the job by getting trained in that subject	✓
A car crashes because of a problem with an embedded computer in a production run	✓

(e) **The first row is an ethical issue and the second is not. If you write an app and give it to your friend to use, it is not an ethical issue at all if they then use it. 2 marks**

Question 1 mark scheme

(a) 1 mark for each marking point, 1 mark for each related example (to max. 8).
▷ Cultural issues, e.g. religious beliefs in the country/use of inappropriate images
▷ Issues of privacy, e.g. monitoring of social media rules may differ
▷ Disability/accessibility issues, e.g. issues with font size/colour/use of images
▷ Political freedom, e.g. countries may have different rules on access to information and ideas
▷ Respecting of intellectual property/ideas, e.g. copyright rules vary by country

(b) The discussion should include subjects such as the following (1 mark each, to max. 8):

Positive:
▷ Looking for new ways to use a program or computer.
▷ Finding alternative ways to work around (programming) bugs.

▷ Finding/exposing security risks software/websites…
▷ …and warning the general public.
▷ Testing out the security of systems.

Negative:
▷ Looking for weaknesses/backdoors in a system…
▷ …in order to steal personal/private data.
▷ Attempting to break a computer system.

(c) 1 mark for each correctly inserted tick.

	✓ if an ethical issue
Your boss can read your work-related and your private emails sent during work time	✓
You have written a new app and given a copy to your friend who is using it without paying for it	
A teacher of a new subject has a responsibility to make sure they can do the job by getting trained in that subject	✓
A car crashes because of a problem with an embedded computer in a production run	✓

Question 2
Student A

(a) If people work at home, they don't have to drive to work using fuel and, at the office, less space is needed so less fuel to keep the office warm and less lighting is needed.

People working for companies that have different offices in the world can use video conferencing, making it unnecessary to use air travel.

Those benefits need to be set against the amount of electricity that all computers use and all of the mobile devices that need charging all the time. Also when computers are changed so often these days, they need to be thrown away and that causes problems.

ⓔ **No mark is awarded for the last point, as the problems caused need to be stated. 5 marks**

(b) (i) Cyberbullying is being horrible to someone or threatening them when on the internet probably using social media.

(ii) Trolling is when someone tries to get a strong response from someone famous so they can publish it in the papers and earn money from it.

ⓔ **For trolling, it doesn't say how, i.e. by posting comments, so this student loses a mark. 3 marks**

Question 2
Student B

(a) People don't have to travel to work any more so they don't use fuel for cars, trains or undergrounds. They can communicate by email without sending letters that use paper and the cost of the postman driving around to deliver them.

ⓔ **The second sentence is a good answer, but it is still worth only 1 mark as 'fuel' has already gained a mark. 2 marks**

(b) (i) Leaving nasty messages on the internet or on Facebook.

ⓔ **This student gets full marks for cyberbullying, but has not answered the second part of the question. 2 marks**

Question 2 mark scheme

(a) 1 mark for each of the following points (to max. 6):

Benefits

People working from home:
⟫ Reduces commuting so less fuel.
⟫ Less office space necessary/saves heating more office space.

Using email/working electronically:
⟫ Less printing paper/less printing ink.

People can use electronic communication systems:
⟫ Any reasonable example such as VoIP, video conferencing etc.
⟫ Less need to travel to meet each other.
⟫ Less fuel used.

Drawbacks

Energy consumption:
⟫ Use of electricity to charge mobile devices/needed by computers.

Technology waste:
⟫ May contain substances poisonous to the environment.
⟫ Habit of constantly updating technology leads to more waste/more fuel to deal with waste.
⟫ If not recycled will go into ground as landfill.

(b) 1 mark for each of the following points:
    (i) ⟫ Abusing another with insults/threats/messages/hurtful remarks…
       ⟫ …over the internet. (Must say over the internet or on the internet for the second mark.)
    (ii) ⟫ Trying to get an emotional comment from somebody (a well-known person)…
       ⟫ …by posting intentionally provocative messages and comments.

Question 3
Student A

(a) Open source software means it is in the public domain and may be used without a licence.

(e) **This is a correct response. 1 mark**

(b) (i)

Advantages	Disadvantages
You can use the source code to change it	You may or may not get updates
You don't need a licence	There won't be any help available or maintenance
It can be worked on so you could make it meet your needs better	

(ii)

Advantages	Disadvantages
If there is a problem, you can probably use customer services	It costs a lot to buy licences
It will have been tested so should work OK	It may not be quite what you want
You get updates that you can just download	You don't get to see the source code, so you can't change it

(e) **The responses are worded well enough to match the requirements of the mark scheme, but this student has listed only two disadvantages for part (i). 11 marks**

(c)

	Proprietary	Open source
Mozilla Firefox		✓
Linux		✓
MS Office	✓	
Adobe Photoshop	✓	
Apache		✓
WordPress		✓

(e) **All the rows are correct. 6 marks**

Question 3
Student B

(a) This means anyone can use it.

(e) **This response shows limited knowledge of what is meant by public domain software. No mark is awarded.**

(b) (i)

Advantages	Disadvantages
You can change it if you want	You don't get free updates like if you had paid for the software
It doesn't cost anything	It may not have been tested out enough and may not work

(ii)

Advantages	Disadvantages
It will work properly because it has been tested	You have to buy it and it is dear
You get free updates of the software to download	
You buy it in a shop or online	

ⓔ The wording of the response is enough to meet the criteria. Not all possible advantages and disadvantages have been listed. **8 marks**

(c)

	Proprietary	Open source
Mozilla Firefox	✓	
Linux		✓
MS Office	✓	
Adobe Photoshop	✓	
Apache		✓
WordPress	✓	✓

ⓔ The first and last rows are incorrect. **4 marks**

Question 3 mark scheme

(a) When the source code of software is made freely available for anyone to download, edit, recompile and redistribute.

(b) 1 mark for each of the following points (to max. 12).

(i)

Advantages	Disadvantages
It is possible to see the source code so changes can be made	Updates usual in other software may not be available/regular
It is (likely to be) free/there is no need to buy a licence to use it	There may be security issues because of lack of security updates/fixes
It can be worked on and improved so may be very good	There is usually no maintenance contract

(ii)

Advantages	Disadvantages
There is recourse if there is a problem	It may be expensive/you have to buy a licence to use it
It is thoroughly tested	It may not serve the needs of the user exactly
There are regular updates	Source code not available/you only get the compiled code
Customers can buy 'off the shelf'	

(c)   1 mark for each row completed correctly.

	Proprietary	**Open source**
Mozilla Firefox		✓
Linux		✓
MS Office	✓	
Adobe Photoshop	✓	
Apache		✓
WordPress		✓

Hints and tips

Don't tick both columns in any row.

Question 4
Student A

(a)   You must not:

>> access computer material without permission

>> look at someone else's files

>> access computer material without permission with intent to commit criminal offences

>> change computer data without permission

ⓔ **The responses in the first and second bullet points are essentially the same. 3 marks**

(b)

Data Protection Act	Organisations that store personal data on a computer system must have processes and security mechanisms
Health and Safety at Work Act	Employers are responsible for appropriate working conditions of staff
Data Protection Act	If you store personal details about others, they must be kept secure
Copyright, Designs and Patents Act	It is illegal to use software unless you buy the appropriate licence
Computer Misuse Act	It is illegal to alter data without permission

(c)   Personal information must be fairly and lawfully processed.

Personal information must be processed for the declared purposes.

Personal information must not be too much.

Personal information must be accurate and up to date.

Personal information must not be kept when you don't need it any more.

Personal information must be processed in line with the data subjects' rights.

Personal information must be kept secure.

Personal information must not be transferred to other countries that don't have a proper Data Protection Act.

ⓔ **Every line of the response is correct, without having to use legal terminology. 8 marks**

Question 4
Student B

(a) Don't access computer material without permission.

Don't hack into a bank's computer.

ⓔ **Two points are given. 2 marks**

(b)

DPA	Organisations that store personal data on a computer system must have processes and security mechanisms
Health and Safety	Employers are responsible for appropriate working conditions of staff
DPA	If you store personal details about others, they must be kept secure
Copyright Act	It is illegal to use software unless you buy the appropriate licence
Computer Misuse Act	It is illegal to alter data without permission

ⓔ **This student must state each Act in full and include the word 'Act'. Only the final row is correct. 1 mark**

Question 4 mark scheme

(a) 3 marks from:
- ➢ Accessing computer material without permission/looking at someone else's files...
- ➢ ...and with intent to commit criminal offences (e.g. hacking into a bank's computer).
- ➢ Alter or change computer data without permission.
- ➢ Write a virus to destroy data belonging to someone else.

(b) 1 mark for each row completed correctly.

Data Protection Act/GDPR	Organisations that store personal data on a computer system must have processes and security mechanisms
Health and Safety at Work Act	Employers are responsible for appropriate working conditions of staff
Data Protection Act	If you store personal details about others, they must be kept secure
Copyright, Designs and Patents Act	It is illegal to use software unless you buy the appropriate licence
Computer Misuse Act	It is illegal to gain unauthorised access to a computer system and alter data without permission

(c) 1 mark for each of the following points:
- ➢ Personal information must be fairly and lawfully processed/used fairly and lawfully.
- ➢ Personal information must be processed for limited purposes/used for specifically stated purposes.
- ➢ Personal information must be adequate, relevant and not excessive.
- ➢ Personal information must be accurate and up to date.
- ➢ Personal information must not be kept for longer than is necessary.
- ➢ Personal information must be processed in line with the data subjects' rights/handled according to a person's data protection rights.

▷ Personal information must be secure/kept safe and secure.
▷ Personal information must not be transferred to other countries without adequate protection/ not transferred outside the European Economic Area without adequate protection.

Question 5
Student A

(a) It is a licence that allows people the right to share, use or build on a work created by an author.

ⓔ **This is a correct response. 1 mark**

(b) Every CC licence has to be given an appropriate credit and the person granting the CC licence can't change their mind later.
CC licences apply to the world.
There are possibly six different types of CC licences.

ⓔ **This is a full and accurate response. 4 marks**

Question 5
Student B

(a) It stands for Creative Commons Licence.

ⓔ **This student has not read the question carefully, so no mark is awarded.**

(b) With a CC licence you always have to credit the person who wrote it and if you keep to the terms of the licence they cannot have it taken away from you.

ⓔ **This student makes three good points. 3 marks**

Question 5 mark scheme

(a) It is a licence that allows people the right to share, use or build on a work created by an author.

(b) 4 marks from:
▷ Every CC licence has to be given appropriate credit.
▷ The person granting you the CC licence may not revoke it…
▷ …as long as you are following the terms of the licence.
▷ There are a possible six CC licences…
▷ …and they apply worldwide.
▷ The licence, once granted, lasts as long as the copyright on the work…
▷ …as long as the licence is used properly.
Marking points starting with … MUST have the previous marking point correct to gain the mark.

Question 6
Student A

(a) 1 Governments
2 Local authorities
3 School
4 Doctors

e **This response is enough for full marks. 4 marks**

(b) Yes

e **This is the correct answer. 1 mark**

(c) Computer files, emails and letters.

e **This answer is correct. 3 marks**

Question 6
Student B

(a) 1 Doctors
2 Schools
3 Teachers
4 Local county council

e **Points 1 and 2 are correct; 3 is incorrect and 4 meets criterion 2 in the mark scheme for local authorities. 3 marks**

(b) No

e **This is incorrect. The Act is retrospective. No mark is awarded.**

(c) Things held on computer. Printed letters.

e **Only two responses have been given. 'Things held on computer' is not specific enough but 'printed letters' is correct. 1 mark**

Question 6 mark scheme

(a) 4 marks from:
- (central) government
- local authorities
- government departments
- (state) schools/colleges/universities
- police (force)
- hospitals/medical surgeries/doctors/opticians/dentists
- national archives

Or any other valid response.

(b) The correct answer is yes.

(c) 3 marks from:
> printed documents
> computer files
> letters
> emails
> photographs
> sound or video recordings

Or any other appropriate response. Look for types of document.

Component 2: Computational thinking, algorithms and programming

Question 1

Student A

(a) Set index to 0 and found to false
     Input search item
     Repeat until index = 10
     If item(index) = search item set found to false
     Increment index
     Report found

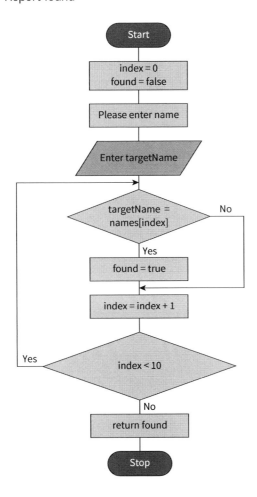

@ Although this design will produce the correct result, it loses a mark because it is inefficient. This is because even if it finds the target name at the first element, it will continue to check all the other elements. **5 marks**

(b) ≫ The list of numbers is split into two sub-lists of about the same size.

≫ These sub-lists are then split again until the sub-lists contain a single number.

≫ Two adjoining sub-lists are merged and sorted.

≫ This continues until all the numbers are in one list. The list is now sorted.

ℯ **This student answers as a list of bullet points, which can be a useful method when defining steps. 5 marks**

(c)
```
procedure bubblesort (listOfNames, numberOfElements)
    i = 0
    j = 0
    while j < numberOfElements
      while i < numberOfElements
        if listOfNames [ i ] > listOfNames [ i + 1 ]
          tempName = listOfNames [ i ]
          listOfNames [ i ] = listOfNames [ i + 1 ]
          listOfNames [ i + 1 ] = tempName
        endif
        i ++
      endwhile
      j ++
    endwhile
endprocedure
```

ℯ **This is a good answer, but this student also needs to make the code more efficient by remembering that after each inner-loop cycle the highest name is at the end. 4 marks**

(d) For each item in the list, move it left until the item to the right of it is bigger.

ℯ **This student covers two marking points in the mark scheme well. It is not clear from the answer that the item is placed in the correct position before the next item is copied, so they do not gain marking point 4. 2 marks**

Question 1
Student B

(a) Input search item

If item(index) = search item found = true

index = index+1

if index = 10 report found

else go to step 2

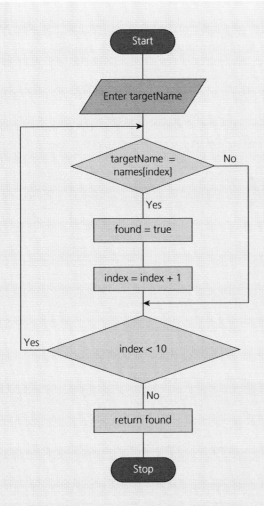

(e) **The value for the array index or the Boolean flag has not been initialised. Although some programming languages will do this automatically, you must not assume that this occurs. Again, the mark for efficiency is not awarded because all elements are checked regardless of the target name already being found. 4 marks**

(b) Divide, conquer and combine steps. Divide the list of numbers into two lists. Conquer by breaking the lists again into two lists. Combine the lists together, sorting as you go.

(e) **This student has used a good method of remembering the steps but lacks enough detail to get all the marks (for example, marking point 3 in the mark scheme). 3 marks**

(c)
```
procedure bubblesort (listOfNames, numberOfElements)
   i = 0
   j = 0
   while j < numberOfElements
     while i < numberOfElements
       if listOfNames [ i ] > listOfNames [ i + 1 ]
         tempName = listOfNames [ i ]
         listOfNames [ i ] = listOfNames [ i + 1 ]
         listOfNames [ i + 1 ] = tempName
       endif
     i = i + 1
     j = j + 1
   endwhile
endprocedure
```

(e) Again, the code is inefficient but this student has also missed out the endwhile of the inner loop, which means that due to their indentation the inner loop is infinite. **3 marks**

(d) The old array is copied into a new array with the data now sorted.

(e) This student has the basic concept that an extra array is required and this array contains the sorted data, but does not mention any of the steps needed. No marks are awarded.

Question 1 mark scheme

(a) 1 mark for each of the following points:
- Initialisation of index to zero (and found).
- Input of target name.
- Checking if target name found.
- Looping around all ten array elements…
- …or stopping loop when target name found.
- Return of correct value.

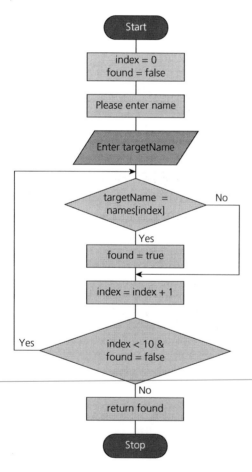

(Note this is an example flowchart and there are other possibilities, the shape of the boxes used in the flowchart are not important, it is the logic that is to be assessed).

(b) 1 mark for each of the following points:
- Divide the unsorted list into roughly two parts.
- Keep dividing the sub-lists…
- …until each one is only one item in length.

> Now merge the sub-lists back into a list twice their size, at the same time sorting items into order.

> Keep merging the sub-lists until the full list is complete once again.

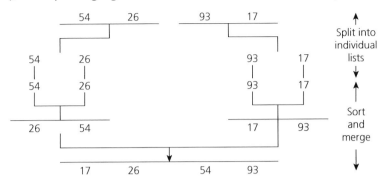

Hints and tips

A diagram is a good alternative way of explaining a method for this type of question.

(c) 1 mark for each part of the code identified by the curly brackets.

```
procedure bubblesort (listOfNames, numberOfElements)
  i = 0
  j = 0
  while j < numberOfElements
    while i < numberOfElements - j }
      if listOfNames [ i ] > listOfNames [ i + 1 ] }
        tempName = listOfNames [ i ] }

        listOfNames [ i ] = listOfNames [ i + 1 ]
        listOfNames [ i + 1 ] = tempName
      endif

      i = i + 1
    endwhile
    j = j + 1
  endwhile
endprocedure
```

Hints and tips

If in doubt about layout/key words, look at the way the question and other questions in the paper are formatted.

(d) 1 mark for each of the following points:
> Starting from the beginning, for each item in turn…
> …move it left (or shift the items to the left of it, right)…
> …until the item is bigger than the one to the left of it…
> …or it is the first item.
> When this has been done for all items, the list is sorted.

Question 2
Student A

(a)
```
procedure displayMenu( )
   exit = false
   do
     print("1. Enter score. ")
     print("2. Display Progress")
     print("3. Exit")
     option = input("Enter option: ")
     switch option:
       case 1:
         enterScore( )
       case 2:
         TeamProgress( )
       case 3:
         exit = true
       default:
         print("Unrecognised selection")
     endswitch
   until exit == true
endprocedure
```

🅔 This student makes good use of the switch statement, which works well with menu options. The mark lost was for marking point 5 in the mark scheme, as they have written TeamProgress rather than teamProgress. This may seem harsh, but most programming languages are case sensitive, so they could be two different procedures in a program. **6 marks**

(b)
```
procedure enterScore( )
   hisTeam = 10
   otherTeam = 10
   do
     homeOrAway = input("Was game played at home or away?")
     homeOrAway = homeOrAway.upper
   until homeOrAway == "H" OR homeOrAway =="A"
   while hisTeam > 9
     hisTeam = input("His team score:")
   endwhile
   while otherTeam > 9
     otherTeam = input(" Other team score:")
   endwhile
   matchDetails = homeOrAway + hisTeam +":" + otherTeam
   teamFile = openWrite("myTeam.dat")
   teamFile.writeLine(matchDetails)
   teamFile.close()
endprocedure
```

🅔 On the whole this is a good answer, but it allowed a negative number to be input for score (marking point 3 in the mark scheme) and did not cast the scores when concatenating (marking point 6). It should be noted that some languages will do the casting automatically, but you need to include casting. **6 marks**

(c)
```
procedure teamProgress( )
   teamPoints = 0
   goalDiff = 0
   teamFile = openRead ("myTeam.dat")
   while NOT myFile.endOfFile()
     matchDetails = teamFile.readLine()
     playedWhere = matchDetails.substring(0,1)
     homeScore = int(matchDetails.substring(1,1))
     awayScore = int(matchDetails.substring(3,1)
     if homeScore == awayScore then
       teamPoints = teamPoints + 1
     elseif playedWhere == "H" then
       if homeScore > awayScore then
         teamPoints = teamPoints + 3
         goalDiff = goalDiff + homeScore - awayScore
       else
         goalDiff = goalDiff + homeScore - awayScore
       endif
     elseif awayScore > homeScore then
       teamPoints = teamPoints + 3
       goalDiff = goalDiff + awayScore - homeScore
     else
       goalDiff = goalDiff + awayScore - homeScore
     endif
   endwhile
   closeFile
   print("Total points is ",teamPoints)
   print("The goal difference is ",goalDiff)
endprocedure
```

(e) The only parts that are incorrect are that this student has missed a closing bracket off the end of int(matchDetails.substring(3,1)) and on the closeFile they forgot to say which file they are closing. **6 marks**

Question 2
Student B

(a)
```
procedure displayMenu( )
   exit = false
   do
     print("1. Enter score. ")
     print("2. Display Progress")
     print("3. Exit")
     option = input("Enter option: ")
     if option = 1 then
       enterScore( )
     elseif option = 2 then
       teamProgress( )
     else
       exit = true
     endif
   until exit = true
endprocedure
```

(e) This student does not get marking point 3 in the mark scheme, as an invalid entry will cause the program to exit. Also, they do not gain marking point 4 because they say set option to 1 (single =) rather than is it equal to (double =). Follow through was allowed, so they gain marking point 5. **5 marks**

(b)
```
procedure enterScore( )
   hisTeam = 10
   otherTeam = 10
   do
      homeOrAway = input("Was game played at home or away? ")
   until homeOrAway == "H" OR homeOrAway == "A"
   while hisTeam > 9 OR hisTeam < 0
      hisTeam = input(" His team score: ")
   while otherTeam > 9 OR otherTeam < 0
   otherTeam = input(" His team score: ")
   matchDetails = homeOrAway + hisTeam + ":" + otherTeam
   teamFile = openWrite("myTeam.dat")
   teamFile.writeLine(matchDetails)
endprocedure
```

(e) This student did not understand what is required. They did not convert Home/Away to uppercase (marking point 2 in the mark scheme). Although the validation picks up the correct range for score, an endwhile is missing and the indentation does not indicate where the endwhile is. They did not cast the scores when concatenating (marking point 6) and did not close the file (marking point 7). **4 marks**

(c)
```
procedure teamProgress( )
   teamPoints = 0
   goalDiff = 0
   teamFile = open ("myTeam.dat")
   while NOT myFile.endOfFile()
      matchDetails = teamFile.readLine()
      playedWhere = matchDetails.substring(1,1)
      homeScore = matchDetails.substring(2,1)
      awayScore = matchDetails.substring(4,1)
      if homeScore == awayScore then
         teamPoints = teamPoints + 1
      elseif playedWhere == "H" then
         if homeScore > awayScore then
            teamPoints = teamPoints + 3
            goalDiff = goalDiff + homeScore - awayScore
         else
            goalDiff = goalDiff + homeScore - awayScore
         endif
      elseif awayScore > homeScore then
         teamPoints = teamPoints + 3
         goalDiff = goalDiff + awayScore - homeScore
      else
         goalDiff = goalDiff + awayScore - homeScore
      endif
   endwhile
   closeFile
   print("Total points is ",teamPoints)
   print("The goal difference is ",goalDiff)
endprocedure
```

(e) This student has forgotten that arrays start at 0 and that when reading from a test file you need to cast when getting a denary number. Although they have got the three parts of matchDetails wrong, they get a mark for follow through on awayScore = ... Again, they forgot to say which file they are closing. **4 marks**

Question 2 mark scheme

(a) 1 mark for each of the following points:
  - The main menu is displayed (at least once).
  - Iteration of the main menu continues…
  - …until only option 3 is selected.
  - Correctly calls enterScore().
  - Correctly calls teamProgress().
  - Correct use of indentation.
  - Meaningful variable name used and correctly initialised.

Example program:
```
procedure displayMenu( )
  exit = false
  option = 0
  do
    print("1. Enter score. ")
    print("2. Display Progress")
    print("3. Exit")
    option = input("Enter option: ")
    if option == 1 then
      enterScore()
    elseif option == 2 then
      teamProgress()
    elseif option == 3 then
      exit = true
    endif
  until exit == true
endprocedure
```

(b) 1 mark for each of the following points:
  - Home or Away entered and…
  - …changed to uppercase and validated to either H or A.
  - Team scores entered and validated to range 0 to 9.
  - Match details concatenated together…
  - …in correct format and…
  - …casting used on score to convert to string.
  - Open file and close file.
  - Write to file.

Example program:
```
procedure enterScore( )
  hisTeamScore = 0
  opposingTeamScore = 0
  playedWhere = "Z"
  do
    playedWhere = input("Was game home or away? ")
    playedWhere = playedWhere.upper
  until playedWhere == "H" OR playedWhere == "A"
  do
    hisTeamScore = input(" His team score: ")
  until hisTeamScore >=0 AND hisTeamScore <=9
  do
    opposingTeamScore = input(" Opposing team score: ")
  until opposingTeamScore >=0 AND opposingTeamScore <=9
  matchDetails = playedWhere + str(hisTeamScore) + ":" + str(opposingTeamScore)
  teamFile = openWrite("myTeam.dat")
  teamFile.writeLine(matchDetails)
  teamFile.close()
endprocedure
```

(c)   1 mark for each of the following correct entries:

```
procedure teamProgress( )
  teamPoints = 0
  goalDiff = 0
  teamFile = openRead ("myTeam.dat")
  while NOT myFile.endOfFile()
    matchDetails = teamFile.readLine()
    playedWhere = matchDetails.substring(0,1)
    homeScore = int(matchDetails.substring(1,1))
    awayScore = int(matchDetails.substring(3,1))
    if homeScore == awayScore then
      teamPoints = teamPoints + 1
    elseif playedWhere == "H" then
      if homeScore > awayScore then
        teamPoints = teamPoints + 3
        goalDiff = goalDiff + homeScore - awayScore
      else
        goalDiff = goalDiff + homeScore - awayScore
      endif
    elseif awayScore > homeScore then
      teamPoints = teamPoints + 3
      goalDiff = goalDiff + awayScore - homeScore
    else
      goalDiff = goalDiff + awayScore - homeScore
    endif
  endwhile
  closefile teamFile
  print("Total points is ",teamPoints)
  print("The goal difference is ",goalDiff)
endprocedure
```

2.2 Programming techniques

Question 1
Student A

(a) Sequence is where the lines of code are executed one after another. An example is:

```
a = b + c
print("result is " + a)
```

Iteration is where a block of code is executed a number of times till it reaches its end condition:

```
do
age = input("Enter age: ")
while age <=15
```

Selection is where a block of code is executed or not depending on a condition which is checked:

```
if age >=17
print(" Apply driving licence")
endif
```

(e) **This is a good basic answer with examples (they have missed the then off the if statement). Although the question is not testing your pseudocode knowledge, it is always good to use the correct format. 9 marks**

(b) The firstName and surname fields are picked from the file studentList and those that have a candidateNumber greater than 1500 and are also in class 4F will be shown.

(e) **The SQL is explained step by step. 4 marks**

(c) SELECT * FROM studentList

WHERE class LIKE '4_' OR surname LIKE '%z%'

(e) **The end semicolon is missed off. Look at any examples given in the paper. 4 marks**

Question 1
Student B

(a) Sequence. The lines of code are run one by one. In order like line 10, 11 and 12. An example would be:

```
10 price = input("Price");
11 qty = input("quantity")
12 total = price * qty
```

Loop. Block of code is executed a number of times:

```
for i = 0 to 5
  print(array[i])
next i
```

Selection. Where lines of code are executed or not depending on a condition:

```
if total < 40 then
postage = total * 0.1
endif
```

(e) The wording of the first sentence in the sequence answer is vague, but the following sentence makes it clear. The marks were lost in the Iteration answer, as this student did not state iteration and gave no indication of the end condition. **7 marks**

(b) Where the candidateNumber is more than 1500 and is also in class 4F their firstName and surname are displayed. So it lists all the forenames and surnames of students that meet the WHERE.

(e) Most parts are answered correctly except that this student has not mentioned the name of the file. **3 marks**

(c) SELECT * FROM studentList

WHERE class LIKE '4*' OR surname LIKE '*z*';

(e) This student has not used the _ or % in the LIKE part of the statement. **3 marks**

Question 1 mark scheme

(a) For each construct, award 1 mark for the name, 1 mark for the description and 1 mark for an example. For example:

Name	Sequence	Selection	Iteration
Description	The (two or more code) statements are performed one after another in a linear way	Depending on a condition, (one or more code) statements are performed or not	One or more code statements are performed in a loop a number of times or until an end condition is met
Example	name = input("What is your name?") print("Hello " + name)	if a > b then print("a is greater than b") endif	for i = 0 to 9 print(i) next i

(b) 1 mark for each of the following points:
  ▷ The firstName and surname columns are selected…
  ▷ …from the studentList file.
  ▷ Those students where the candidateNumber is greater than 1500…
  ▷ …and their class is 4F will be displayed.

(c) 1 mark for each of the following points (to max. 4):
  ▷ SELECT * FROM studentList
  ▷ WHERE class LIKE '4_'
  ▷ OR
  ▷ surname LIKE '%z%'

Here is a full example:

SELECT * FROM studentList

WHERE class LIKE '4_' OR surname LIKE '%z%';

2.3 Producing robust programs

Question 1
Student A

(a) A syntax error is where the code does not follow the rules of the programming language. Likely causes of the mistakes are spelling key words incorrectly, missing brackets out or incorrect placing of endifs etc.

(e) **This student shows a good understanding of syntax errors. 3 marks**

(b) A logic error is when you get an output from the program that was not intended. The likely cause is that you have the logic wrong, for example by using a > instead of a >= condition.

(e) **The first sentence could contain more details, but overall it is worth the mark for marking point 1 in the mark scheme. 2 marks**

(c) This testing is carried out as you are writing the code, usually one function at a time. The outcome of the testing can be used to change the code if errors are found or maybe layout problems.

(e) **To gain the third and fourth marks, it must be clear that you are writing about feedback. 4 marks**

Question 1
Student B

(a) Syntax error is when you have spelling mistakes, such as prinf when you should have put printf, also you may have missed a bracket off.

(e) **This student does not get marking point 1 in the mark scheme, as they do not mention that it is when the code does not follow the rules of the language. 2 marks**

(b) This happens when you write the code incorrectly. You may have put a call to a function in the wrong place.

(e) **The description is not clear enough for marking point 1 in the mark scheme, but the example is good. The student could also have said 'put a call to the wrong function'. 1 mark**

(c) As we write the program, we test it and do changes as we go along.

(e) **This student gains the first mark, but does not make it clear that they are using the outcome from the testing to make changes if required. 1 mark**

Question 1 mark scheme

(a) 1 mark for 'A syntax error is when the code does not follow the rules of the language/mistake in the way the code is written.'

Plus 2 marks from:
- The cause can be spelling errors (of keywords), e.g. prinf instead of print.
- The cause can be the incorrect use of punctuation/brackets/terminators.
- Words/symbols used in the incorrect order e.g. 4 + 5 = x
- The cause can be the incorrect use of capital letters, e.g. Print instead of print.

(b) 1 mark for each of the following points:
  ▷ A logic error is when the program produces an unintended or undesired output or behaviour.
  ▷ An example is if a > b then when it should have been if a < b then. Accept any reasonable example.

(c) 1 mark for each of the following points:
  ▷ Testing the code as it is created…
  ▷ …could be line by line or a section at a time (function or procedure).
  ▷ The outcome of the testing is fed back and…
  ▷ …used to alter the code if required.

Question 2
Student A

(a)

Test data		Type of test	Expected outcome
x	**y**		
12	10	Valid	Valid entry
15	12	In range	Valid entry
0	1	Out of range	Invalid entry
Null	Null	Null	Invalid entry
Pit	Stop	Invalid	Invalid entry

ℯ **All correct. 4 marks**

(b) To check that the program works correctly and that we are unable to break it. We test a program with the aim of trying to prove it fails rather than trying to prove it works.

ℯ **This is a good answer as we should always be looking at proving the robustness of our code. 2 marks**

Question 2
Student B

(a)

Test data		Type of test	Expected outcome
x	**y**		
12	10	Valid	Valid entry
10	1	In range	Valid entry
18	12	Out of range	Invalid entry
Null	Null	Null	Invalid entry
D	J	Invalid	Invalid entry

ℯ **'In range' is where we look at the maximum and minimum values that should be input. The value for x should be either 1 or 15. 3 marks**

(b) To make sure that the program works as expected.

ℯ **This student does not mention checking to see if the program works under all inputs. 1 mark**

Question 2 mark scheme

(a) With this type of question there will multiple possible right answers. 1 mark for each valid set of test data and expected outcome, to a maximum of 4 marks. Suggested response:

Test data		Type of test	Expected outcome
x	**y**		
12	10	Valid	Valid entry
1	1	In range	Valid entry
16	12	Out of range	Invalid entry
15	Null	Null	Invalid entry
T	1	Invalid	Invalid entry

(b) 1 mark for each of the following points:
  ≫ To see that the program works as expected (by using obvious input data).
  ≫ To see if we can break the program (by using extreme test data).

Question 3
Student A

(a) The program validates the input to check that it is reasonable and sensible. It does this by making sure that data is within certain limits or formats.

🅮 **Formats can be taken as rules because rules define the format. 2 marks**

(b) Format check – this checks that the data contain the right characters and symbols.
Presence check – this makes sure we have entered data in a required field.
Lookup table – checks a table to see if it is a valid value.
Check digit – used to check.

🅮 **This student loses a mark from format check because the definition reads as verification and another mark is lost from the last response because they did not complete the definition. 6 marks**

Question 3
Student B

(a) It checks that the data is within acceptable limits.

🅮 **This student explains how it does it, but not what validation is. 1 mark**

(b) Range check makes sure that the data values are in a given range.
Spell check.
Presence check makes sure that a data value has been entered.
Check sum
Format check checks that the data is in the right format so time would be hh:mm:ss.
Lookup table.

(e) This student gets 2 marks each for the first and third answers. They get only 1 mark for the 'Spell check' response, because they have not provided a definition, and no marks for 'Check sum'. They get no marks for the last two responses because the question asked for only four responses. If students provide a list greater than what is required, the extra responses will not be marked, even if they would have produced better marks. **5 marks**

Question 3 mark scheme

(a) 1 mark for each of the following points:
  ▷ Validation is a check made by a computer to ensure that the data entered is sensible or reasonable.
  ▷ It attempts to ensure that it is within certain limits or rules.

(b) Mark in pairs. Max 8 marks:
  ▷ Format check…
  ▷ …checks the data is in the right format (such as dd/mm/yyyy).
  ▷ Presence check…
  ▷ …checks that data has been entered into a field (i.e. the entry is not null).
  ▷ Range check…
  ▷ …checks that a value falls within the specified range (i.e. 1 to 10).
  ▷ Lookup table…
  ▷ …checks to see if it is an acceptable value in a table.
  ▷ Spell check…
  ▷ …checks to see if a word is in a dictionary.
  ▷ Check digit…
  ▷ …checks the other digits are correct.

2.4 Computational logic

Question 1
Student A

(a) Binary form has two possible states whereas denary requires 10 states.

(e) **Points 1 and 5 in the mark scheme are covered. 2 marks**

A binary state is either TRUE or FALSE, for example voltage present or not.

(e) **Point 3 in the mark scheme is covered. As point 1 has already been given, the mark for point 2 is awarded. 2 marks**

Binary computers are less complicated to produce than denary systems.

(e) **The mark for point 3 has already been given, so the mark for point 4 is awarded. 1 mark**

(b)

A	B	P
FALSE	FALSE	FALSE
FALSE	TRUE	TRUE
TRUE	FALSE	TRUE
TRUE	TRUE	TRUE

(e) These are the correct answers. **2 marks**

(c)

A	B	Q
FALSE	FALSE	FALSE
FALSE	TRUE	FALSE
TRUE	FALSE	TRUE
TRUE	TRUE	FALSE

(e) These are the correct answers. **4 marks**

(d)

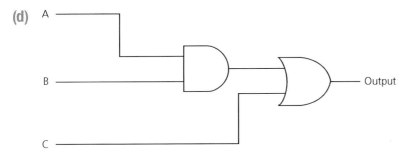

(e) This diagram is correct. **4 marks**

Question 1
Student B

(a) Binary form has two possible states, which can be either TRUE or FALSE, for example voltage charge present or not.

(e) **This student covers points 1, 2 and 3 in the mark scheme. 3 marks**

Denary computers are very complicated to produce.

(e) **No marks for this sentence, they have not given point 5, so they are unable to gain the mark for point 6. Also, it is not clear with what it is being compared. 3 marks**

(b)

A	B	P
FALSE	FALSE	FALSE
FALSE	TRUE	TRUE
TRUE	FALSE	TRUE
TRUE	TRUE	FALSE

(e) **The last entry is incorrect. Although not covered in the specification, this student gives a truth table for an exclusive OR (XOR). 1 mark**

(c)

A	B	Q
FALSE	FALSE	FALSE
FALSE	TRUE	FALSE
TRUE	FALSE	TRUE
TRUE	TRUE	TRUE

(e) **The last entry is incorrect. This student has not applied the NOT gate to input B. 3 marks**

(d)

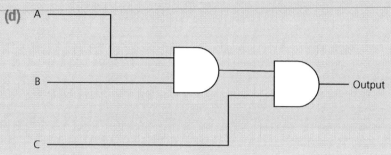

(e) **The AND gate with inputs from A and B is correct. 2 marks**

Question 1 mark scheme

(a) 5 marks from:
- ▷ Binary has two possible states…
- ▷ …TRUE/1 or FALSE/0.
- ▷ So a binary state can be represented by an electrical voltage/current/charge being present or not…
- ▷ …making computer circuits easier to make (by the use of 'switches').
- ▷ In a denary system a switch would have to have 10 possible states…
- ▷ …making circuits much more complicated (and consuming more power).

(b) 1 mark for each correct answer.

A	B	P
FALSE	FALSE	FALSE
FALSE	TRUE	TRUE
TRUE	FALSE	TRUE
TRUE	TRUE	TRUE

(c) 1 mark for each correct answer.

A	B	Q
FALSE	FALSE	FALSE
FALSE	TRUE	FALSE
TRUE	FALSE	TRUE
TRUE	TRUE	FALSE

(d) 1 mark for each of the following points:

  ≫ Use of correct AND gate symbol…
  ≫ …and correct inputs.
  ≫ Use of correct OR gate symbol…
  ≫ …and correct inputs.

Correct logic circuit:

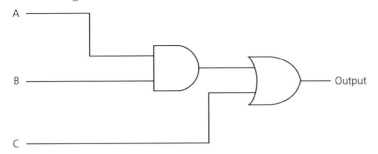

Hints and tips

Look for an input that always gives an output if TRUE and this then indicates that it will be OR'd with the output of the other two inputs.

Question 2
Student A

(a) The mathematical operator MOD gives the remainder when one integer value is divided by another. For example 14 MOD 5 would give a result of 4. In the case of DIV it carries out an integer division. For example 14 DIV 5 would give a result of 2.

ⓔ **This student gets full marks for a correct response. 4 marks**

(b) 24

ⓔ **This student has correctly applied operator precedence. 1 mark**

(c) Items in the brackets are worked out first, which means that they can change the order of precedence. If there are nested brackets, you start calculating from the inner bracket and work outwards to the outer bracket.

ⓔ **This student has covered all points from the mark scheme. 3 marks**

Question 2
Student B

(a) The use of MOD returns the remainder when one number is divided by another, so 14 MOD 5 gives 4.

ⓔ **Although this example does show integer values, no benefit of doubt is given for marking point 1 in the mark scheme, so 1 mark is awarded.**

DIV is used for the division of numbers.

ⓔ **It is not clear whether they are talking about integer values, so only 1 mark is awarded. 2 marks**

(b) 52

ⓔ **This is incorrect as this student has not taken into account operator precedence. No marks are awarded.**

(c) Brackets are used to allow us to change the order in which the calculations take place.
The formula in the brackets is done first.

ⓔ **The student has recognised that the part in brackets takes precedence. 2 marks**

Question 2 mark scheme

(a) 1 mark for each of the following points:
▷ MOD (modulus) gives the remainder when one integer number is divided by another.
▷ For example, 6 MOD 4 would give a value of 2.
▷ DIV (quotient) performs an integer division.
▷ For example, 6 DIV 4 would give a value of 1.

(b) The correct answer is 24, i.e. $14 + 18 - 8$

(c) 1 mark for each of the following points:
▷ Brackets can be used to change order of precedence.
▷ Items in brackets are evaluated first.
▷ Items are evaluated in turn, from innermost to outermost bracket.

2.5 Translators and facilities of languages

Question 1
Student A

(a) A high-level language is made up of human language words, which make it easier for us to read and write. A low-level language is closely related to the design of the machine, which means we can write faster programs, but it is far more difficult to read and write. An example of a high-level language is Python and an example of low-level is machine code.

ⓔ **This is a good answer. 5 marks**

(b) It will take the high-level source code and convert it to machine code so that it will be able to run on the machine.

ⓔ **Full marks for a correct answer. 2 marks**

(c) A compiler takes the whole program and converts it into machine code, with the machine code being saved in a file. Any errors found during translation are not shown until the translation has finished.

ⓔ **This student has not shown that they understand that the program is compiled before execution. 3 marks**

(d) The interpreter. This takes each line of code in turn and translates it into machine code and runs it, before moving on to the next line. The code has to be translated each time the code is run, as it does not create a file. Any errors found are shown.

ⓔ Although the student states that error reporting takes place, they needed to say when. 5 marks

(e) editors

error diagnostics

translator(s)

ⓔ Full marks for a correct response. 3 marks

Question 1
Student B

(a) A low-level language is difficult to read and write as it is in binary, whereas a high-level language is in a human-readable form. Low-level languages are written in machine code. An example of a high level is Java.

ⓔ Machine code is mentioned, although not directly as an example. 3 marks

(b) It will change the high level into binary.

ⓔ It is unclear what is being converted and that it will produce a program rather than just a binary pattern. No marks are awarded.

(c) A compiler takes the code and converts it to binary form that can be run. This binary form is saved in a file. It reports any errors found.

ⓔ Although this student has not explicitly said machine code, the fact that it says 'can be run' is enough for marking point 1 in the mark scheme. The second sentence is enough for the final marking point. However, to show a difference between compiler and interpreter, they should say when the errors are reported. 2 marks

(d) It is an interpreter. It converts one line at a time into machine code and runs it before moving on to the next line. Errors are reported as they are found.

ⓔ This student starts well, but then fails to mention that it does not create a file so needs to be translated each time. 4 marks

(e) editors

error handling

run-time environment

ⓔ Error handling refers to when a program is running and an error occurs, rather than during translation. 2 marks

Question 1 mark scheme

(a) 5 marks from:
- High-level language is easier to read and write/low-level language is harder to read and write.
- Low-level language is close to the design of the machine/processor.
- Low-level language is written in binary/machine code/assembler.
- Programs written in a low-level language tend to be faster.
- Examples: a high-level language is Java/Python (allow any other high-level language) and a low-level language is assembly/machine code.

(b) 2 marks from:
- It converts high-level (source) code into machine/object code…
- …so that it will run on the machine/processor…
- …as a CPU can only 'understand' machine code.

(c) 1 mark for each of the following points:
- A compiler translates the whole program into machine code…
- …before the program can be run.
- Errors/bugs are reported at the end of compilation.
- The machine code is saved and stored in a file separate to the high-level code.

(d) 1 mark for each of the following points (to max. 6):
- It is an interpreter.
- It translates code into machine code, line by line.
- The processor executes each line of code before the interpreter moves on to translate the next one.
- It shows reports as errors as soon as they are found.
- An interpreter does not create an (executable) file.
- The code has to be translated each time the code is run…
- …which requires access to the interpreter.

(e) 3 marks from:
- editors
- error diagnostics
- run-time environment
- translator(s)

Hints and tips

There are many other tools and facilities that can be included within an IDE (such as version control), but it always best that you use the ones in the specification because they will be in the mark scheme.

Question 1
Student A

(a) 01000001

ⓔ This is correct. **1 mark**

(b) 2F

ⓔ This is correct. **1 mark**

(c) Can be held in a nibble (4 bits).

ⓔ This is correct. **1 mark**

(d)   0 1 1 0 1 1 0 1
        0 1 0 1 1 1 0 1
        _____
        1 1 0 0 1 0 1 0
        _____
        1 1 1 1 1   1

ⓔ This is correct. **2 marks**

(e) Check digits are used to check that the input is correct. They do this by a mathematical calculation on the data and checking the value is the same as the check digit. This means that if we have accidentally swapped numbers round, it will tell us there is an error.

ⓔ This is correct. **2 marks**

(f) A character set is a list of the characters that a computer can understand. Each character is given a unique number. The number of characters that a character set can hold depends on the bits allowed. ASCII can have 128 characters and Extended ASCII can have 256 characters.

ⓔ This student has given more information than required but covers all points very well. **3 marks**

Question 1
Student B

(a) 1000001

ⓔ The value is correct, but not held in 8 bits. No marks are awarded.

(b) F2

ⓔ This student transcribes the values probably using the repeated division method. No marks are awarded.

(c) 3 bits will hold a hex digit.

ⓔ An octal value is held in 3 bits. No mark is awarded.

(d) 0 1 1 0 1 1 0 1

     0 1 0 1 1 1 0 1

     ――――――――

     1 1 0 1 1 0 1 0

     ――――――――

     1 1 1 1   1

ⓔ **This student has missed the carry from the right-hand fourth column, but still achieves the 4 LSBs correctly. 1 mark**

(e) Check digits are normally at the end of barcodes and are used to check that the code read is correct. So they are used to pick up errors when data is input.

ⓔ **The last sentence is the opposite of saying it is checking that it is correct. 1 mark**

(f) What characters a computer can understand and recognise. A number is given to a character to say what it is. ASCII is an example of a character set.

ⓔ **The first sentence is just about enough to get the first point from the mark scheme. In the second sentence, 'number' should really say 'unique number'. This student did not read the question correctly. 2 marks**

Question 1 mark scheme

(a) The correct answer is 8 bits represented as the binary pattern 01000001.

Hints and tips
Always check you have the correct number of bits.

(b) The correct answer is 2F.

(c) The correct answer is a nibble/4 bits.

(d) The correct answer is 11001010. 1 mark for each of the following points:
> 4 MSBs correct.
> 4 LSBs correct.

(e) 2 marks from:
> It helps to verify that the number entered is correct.

By providing the answer to a calculation carried out on the rest of the number.
> It helps to check if a transposition error has occurred (two digits swapped round).
> It helps to check if a transcription error has occurred (wrong number entered).

(f) 1 mark for each of the following points:
> A defined list of characters recognised by the computer (hardware and software).
> Each character is represented by a unique number.
> Unicode/Extended ASCII/EBCDIC.

Question 2
Student A

(a) Compression software could be used to make the file sizes smaller by changing attributes such as resolution or colour depth.

🅮 **This is correct. 2 marks**

(b) The two methods are lossy and lossless.

🅮 **This is correct. 2 marks**

(c) I would use lossless as the picture quality is the same as the original and so is the depth of colour. The enlarged image will look better than if I used lossy.

🅮 **This student does not really explain why lossy would be worse in this case. 3 marks**

Question 2
Student B

(a) The files can be made smaller by the use of a compression application.

🅮 **This is a 2-mark question, so this student should have made two good points. 1 mark**

(b) The methods are JPEG and PNG files.

🅮 **Although these use lossy and lossless, the question asked for methods not file formats. No marks are awarded.**

(c) We need to maintain picture quality and colour depth so I would use a PNG file.

🅮 **This student has not stated the compression type, so they do not get marking point 1 in the mark scheme, which means they are unable to get the rest of the marks. No marks are awarded.**

Question 2 mark scheme

(a) 2 marks from:
   ▷ By the use of compression software...
   ▷ ...which reduces the file size…
   ▷ ...and decreases colour depth/resolution.

(b) 1 mark for each of the following points:
   ▷ Lossy
   ▷ Lossless

(c) 1 mark for each of the following points:
   ▷ Lossless
   ▷ Depth of colour is not reduced/original picture quality is maintained/no loss of resolution, so...
   ▷ ...there's no reduction in quality/artifacting that would become visible when the image is enlarged (as there would be with lossy).

Question 3
Student A

(a) A measurement of the sound is sampled at regular intervals and its value is converted into binary and stored in a file for later transfer to her laptop.

ⓔ **This student has covered all the points and has answered in the context of the question. 3 marks**

(b) By decreasing the sample rate, she will decrease the quality of the sound because there are fewer values to make the sound wave. Also, as there are fewer samples the file size will be smaller.

ⓔ **This is correct. 4 marks**

Question 3
Student B

(a) The value of the sound is read at intervals and converted into binary for storage in a file.

ⓔ **'Read' is on the weak side, but enough to get the mark. It is important to mention the time interval between samples. 2 marks**

(b) Decreasing the sample rate will make the file size small, so she will be able to record more birds. The problem is the quality of the sound will be reduced.

ⓔ **This student has not given enough detail to gain the follow-on marks. 2 marks**

Question 3 mark scheme

(a) 3 marks from:
  ▷ The microphone converts the sound to electrical signals.
  ▷ The audio wave height is sampled/measured…
  ▷ …at regular/set intervals.
  ▷ The value at the sampled point is converted into a binary value and stored (in a file).

(b) 1 mark for each of the following points:
  ▷ The sound quality (on replay) will decrease…
  ▷ …because less data are available to recreate the sound wave.
  ▷ The file size will decrease…
  ▷ …because there are fewer samples to store.